FROM MY
Mama's Kitchen®
"Food for the Soul, Recipes for living"

My 9 MOMS
Conversations about Life, Love, and Laughter!

Johnny Tan

From My Mama's Kitchen® Publishing

From My Mama's Kitchen® Publishing
2050 N. Stemmons Fwy, Unit 396
Dallas, Texas 75207-3234

Original Copyright ©2009, Johnny Tan
Current Copyright ©2024, Johnny Tan
From My Mama's Kitchen® is a registered trademark owned by Johnny Tan
All rights reserved.

E-Book: ISBN 978-0-9820235-4-9
Paperback: ISBN 978-0-9820235-5-6
Hardcover: ISBN-978-0-9820235-6-3
Library of Congress Control Number: 2024924834
Original Copyright TXu 1-618-884

Cover and Interior Design: Elizabeth Felker

All rights reserved. No part of this publication may be reproduced, stored in a retrieval system for distribution, or transmitted in any form or by any means, including scanning, photocopying, recording, or other electronic or mechanical methods, without the prior written permission of the publisher, except in the case of brief quotations embodied in critical reviews and specific other noncommercial uses permitted by copyright law. For permission requests, write to the publisher, addressed "Attention: Permission Coordinator," at the address below.

From My Mama's Kitchen® Publishing
2050 N. Stemmons Fwy, Unit 396
Dallas, Texas 75207-3234
USA

First Edition, 2009
15th Anniversary Special Edition, 2024
Printed on acid-free paper.

To:

From:

A page to dedicate this book to someone special.

I dedicate the book to my father, Koon Kim Tan (1923-1981), affectionately called Baba by my sister and me. Your unconditional love, life values, and fathership have forever been a source of excellence in all areas of our family life.

Your resiliency, integrity, and work ethic have always inspired me, and your continuous spiritual presence in my life will always be a comfort to me for the rest of my life.

This book is also lovingly dedicated to all my 9 Moms and Mothers worldwide.

Thank you for your unconditional motherly love, inspiring wisdom, and empowering support in building a better world for others to benefit from and follow!

Contents

Acknowledgments   i
Preface   iii
Introduction   viii

From My Mama's Kitchen

Chapter One   1
Chapter Two   5
Chapter Three   15
Chapter Four   25

Food for the Soul

Chapter Five   31
Chapter Six   45

Recipes for Living

Chapter Seven   59

    1. Time is a luxury we all have   60
    2. The dance of life - are we following, or are we leading?   61
    3. Something Interesting about fortune cookies   63
    4. The essence of making a change   64
    5. Having a balanced approach to everything   65
    6. Being present in the present moment   65
    7. Overcoming Fear   67
    8. The art of being a good listener   68

9. Annual rebirths	70
10. The answers are all around us	72
11. The power of positive visualization	73
12. The various seasons of our life	75
13. The synergy of the heart and the mind	76
14. Living a mindful life	76
15. Character-driven living	77
16. Having a sense of humor in everything we do	78
17. The art of moving forward with our lives	79
18. Creating the right first impression	80
19. The art of planning future success	80
20. The dance of life - the synergy of oneness	82
21. Defining ourselves	84
22. The power of having the right friends and associates	85
23. Inner power - the magic from within	86
24. A purpose-driven life	87
25. Sometimes, a chance encounter can bring great meaning to our lives	88
26. Hearing the rest of the story	90
27. A recipe for writing	91
28. Education will always be part of our life's journey	92
29. The art of turning a job into a career	93
30. Taking the right time-out in life	95

Coming to a Full Circle

Chapter Eight	97

My 9 MOMS - Conversations about Life, Love, and Laughter

Chapter Nine	103

1. Smiling Sows Happiness - Elsa Mae	104
2. Gratitude Cultivates Blessings - Eleanora	105
3. Generosity Reaps Abundance - Carol	106
4. Faith Comforts - Ginger	107
5. Hope Inspires - Nyah	108
6. Love Empowers - Dianne	109
7. Always Lean Towards Heaven - Toni	110
8. Passion is When the Heart Creates, the Mind Formulates - Betty	111
9. Wisdom is about knowing Others. Enlightenment is about knowing Ourselves - Dee	112

Food Recipes

Recipes from Eleanor Carter	123
Recipes from Carol Wisdom	126
Recipe from Dianne Heise	128
Recipe from Ginger White	130
Recipe from Elsa Mae Stevens	133
Recipe from Nyah Tan	135

Acknowledgments

I would like to take this opportunity to express my heartfelt thanks and gratitude to my respective moms— thank you for your vote of confidence and participation in this empowering, heart-centered, and passion-driven project. Your loving support, encouragement, and prayers truly kept me motivated from beginning to end.

To my friends Teresa Velardi, Amb. Dr. Randi D. Ward and From My Mama's Kitchen® Publishing success team members Jessica Trippe and Elizabeth Felker—thank you for your timely support, creativity, and expertly refined finishing touches in making this very special heart-centered and passion-driven book a true gem!

To all my original success team members—Kathleen Tucci, Desiree Jacobsen, Teresa Nguyen, Kelly Hoffman, Jamie Saloff, Sharon K. Garner, Mary Gnetz, Pat Wood, Marjie & Michael Parenteau, the RED iD Agency team, and Megan Goad—thank you for your enthusiasm, expertise, and close support in making my journey of writing and publishing my first book in 2009, an enriching and

FROM MY **Mama'sKitchen**®

satisfying experience.

Finally, to all of you readers, thank you for joining me in honoring our moms for their spiritual and inspirational contributions to making a positive difference in our daily lives by bringing their empowering, unconditional motherly love for us to center stage. It is living a legacy of love at its best!

Preface

Hi, Everyone;

I am excited to share this very special heart-centered and passion-driven book honoring my moms and all mothers worldwide. I can still recall the fun and joyful book signing memories I experienced at the various Barnes and Noble and Independent Bookstores, as well as at the National and Regional Book Exposition Events and Writers Conferences all over the country. Fans were delighted and intrigued to hear a man speak highly of his mom—in my case, 9 Moms!

The number one question people always ask me is, How do I manage to have 9 Moms? Sometimes, before I could begin to answer this question, they would follow up with another one: Is it a blessing or a curse?

My answer is always a blessing, a tremendous blessing. As an adopted child at birth in Melaka, Malaysia, and later in the United States, experiencing the motherly attention I received from my beloved *"8 surrogate moms,"* I must be the luckiest kid on the block! I was fortunate to have my 9 Moms as my teachers, coaches, counselors, and cheerleaders. Their genuine caring support was the gentle push when I was at a stop, a trusted guide when I was rolling, and the loudest cheerers whenever I was inches away from the various finish lines. I am forever grateful for their presence in my life.

Who and where I am Today is the result of the delicate sprinkling of a dash of this, a smidgen of that, and a pinch of these ladies' unconditional motherly teaching, coaching, counseling, and cheerleading over time as I journeyed to discover who I am, why I am here, and what my purpose is. Always looking through the lens of love, they never miss a beat in sharing their motherly wisdom to help me navigate life's challenges and celebrate successes.

Their natural motherly intuition and unconditional love approach to our relationship epitomized this sentiment, *"A Family Experience is Defined by Who Loves Us and Who We Love, rather than by our shared DNA."*

Although there are exceptions to the norm, our personal success begins at home. It is the first classroom we are all enrolled in as we begin our respective life's journey, learning from the University of Life. Our parents, especially moms, are always looking out for us to live our best lives, then and in the future. They are always looking through the lens of love, as we are consciously open to receiving love.

I left Malaysia at 18 to attend college at Louisiana State University. At 33, I successfully led a multigenerational workforce team of 600+ employees as their Chief Operating Officer. For over 12 years, I also served my Baton Rouge community by initiating projects that benefited future generations as chairman of the board and president of several organizations. Later, I became a small business owner and a social entrepreneur in Dallas, Texas.

Although I reached the peak of my personal Mount Everest in my early thirties, I also unexpectedly experienced falling to the bottom of the

Grand Canyon of Life in my late forties. Thanks to my 9 Moms, I made it through safely and with as few scrapes and bruises as possible.

The nine months it took me to write the original *From My Mama's Kitchen—"food for the soul, recipes for a living"*—to honor my 9 Moms were a tremendous treat, as I experienced a *"spiritual awakening."* The educational richness I have accumulated from the relationships I had with my 9 Moms helped me to understand that *"home"* is also within oneself. I have experienced the American dream in a unique way. I came to the United States to earn an engineering degree. Instead, I received an education about the power of relationships, the nature of love, and the meaning of life. Thanks to my 9 Moms, I learned that I could achieve real connections, true love, and success by engaging others with authentic integrity, listening with empathy, and speaking with humility.

I self-published the book in 2009 with the endorsement of the National Association of Mothers' Centers. It won five awards: Mom's Choice Awards, Mr. Dad Seal of Recognition, Publisher's Choice Awards by Family Magazine Group in 2010, and the International Book Awards and National Indie Excellence Book Awards in 2011. The book also made the Amazon Best Seller List in the following categories: Parenting& Family Relationships: Parent and Adult Child, Self Help: Spiritual and Motivational, and Cooking, Food & Wine: Essay, in 2012.

I started From My Mama's Kitchen® Talk Radio to complement the book release. The show amassed over one million listeners. The weekly kitchen table conversations feature *"ordinary people, especially women, doing extraordinary things,"* sharing a common goal of building a better world for everyone. The success of the book launched my third career as

FROM MY **Mama'sKitchen**®

I created From My Mama's Kitchen® Educational platform, advocating the concept of *"Personal Success Begins at Home."* My experiential keynote presentations and workshops help audiences identify and gain a new, fresh perspective on conscious living, working, self-empowerment, and personal leadership in their personal and professional lives. My real-life stories of circumstances, unexpected setbacks, successful rebounds, and arriving at my highest self resonate and connect with audiences and my coaching clients of all ages.

To celebrate and honor the contribution of my 9 Moms, in this 15th anniversary special edition, I created a new ninth chapter titled My 9 MOMS—Conversations About Life, Love, and Laughter. This chapter features 9 New Recipes for Living that have tremendously impacted my life in the last 15 years, complementing the various engaging, entertaining, and enlightening *"timeless recipes for living life"* sprinkled throughout the book.

Respectfully, regardless of where you are in life, I hope the insightful, evergreen nuggets of knowledge and wisdom shared in this book will help you successfully navigate your life journey with plenty of smiles. More importantly, may they rekindle those special, beautiful moments between you and your mom(s), as life and living are about leaving a legacy of love for future generations to benefit from and follow!

With gratitude and blessings always,

Johnny

**2012
Amazon Bestseller List**

Parenting & Family:
Relationships

Self Help: Spiritual &
Motivational

Cooking, Food & Wine:
Essay

FROM MY
Mama's Kitchen®
Inspirations for Better Living

Introduction

Everyone knows the kitchen is a place where our meals are prepped, cooked, and served. However, there are some of us who consider it, as a classroom for learning some of life's most insightful and thought-provoking lessons. After reflecting back on the time spent in the kitchen with my mom over the years, I realized that the kitchen has indeed been both a place for our family meal preparations and also a venue for my mom and me to engage in many meaningful and respectful conversations that have fed and nourished both my physical and spiritual appetites.

I can recall that even if a conversation ends in a disagreement or an argument, just before she leaves me to myself, my mom still pats me on my shoulder as a gentle reminder that she loves me, trusting that this simple loving gesture feeds my soul just as her dishes had fed my physical appetite. It is within this wonderful state of mind that I begin to share with you this seemingly not so Secret—*Secret*.

Growing up with six brothers and sisters working in the rice fields of Malacca, Malaya (present-day Melaka, Malaysia) in the 1930s and 1940s, my mom became an excellent cook for her family through the encouragement and tutelage of her grandmother.

Although the path she took was clearly her decision, many young Malaysian girls at that time were strongly encouraged to enroll in what I've coined as Kitchen 101 as soon as they developed the cognitive ability and sense of responsibility to work with open fire and hot water.

Mom started prepping food at six years old and later became the lead cook for her family at twelve. What began as a genuine curiosity about how to prepare the various meals to feed her family soon became a passion and a fulfillment in contributing to her family's overall well-being. She saw that through her dishes, she was able to ease her family's daily routine of working in the rice fields under the smoldering heat of the tropical sun by putting a smile on each one of their faces and granting an overall feeling of contentment at the dinner table.

Over the years, my mom became the most sought-after auntie by her nephews and nieces—and sister by her siblings—at family gatherings as the special guest cook. I can remember how our home became everyone's favorite destination during the holidays. It seemed that there was a sign above our front door that read, *"Come hungry and leave stuffed and happy."*

Unlike my older sister Rosalind, who did not enjoy cooking at the time, as she was focused on her studies and future career, I looked forward to hanging out with my mom in the kitchen during the school holidays and serving as the official *"family food taster"* for her various dishes. I did not officially learn how to cook until I was 18 years old after leaving for college, and lived on my own halfway around the world in Baton Rouge, Louisiana.

My interest in cooking was sparked by necessity and a longing to eat my favorite Nyonya dishes. Nyonya food is a fusion cuisine derived from the blending of Chinese, Malay, Javanese, and South Indian spices and herbs, resulting in a unique, flavorful food rich in taste and aroma. This cuisine comes from the Peranakans, the culturally rich early Chinese migrants who settled in Penang, Malacca, Singapore, and Indonesia and intermarried the local Malays.

Mom was quick to send me the many spices I needed and was only a phone call away to walk me through the cooking process whenever necessary. Soon, cooking became a time for rest and relaxation at the end of a school day and later at the end of a workday.

In November 1999, my mom was leaving after staying with me for close to six memorable months. Among the many fun things we had done together that summer was to be featured in one of the weekly food sections of *The Advocate,* Louisiana's largest daily newspaper based in Baton Rouge. The feature, titled *"Remembering His Roots,"* focused on Nyonya Cuisine and my special bond with my mom, which had surpassed the physical distance between my life in the United States and her life with my sister and her family in Malaysia.

During my mom's visit, I came to realize that she, after celebrating her seventy-first birthday, was growing older and that her traveling days might be numbered. While trying to find a way to honor her memory, I started to memorize most of my favorite recipes while cooking with her. However, I soon realized that I needed to start writing the various recipes down for future reference, as there were too many to remember. So, I decided to do something special for my sister and me by collecting mom's recipes and writing a family cookbook. I would call it *From My Mama's Kitchen—food for the soul, recipes for living*, to remind me of the various wonderful moments I had spent cooking and conversing with her in the kitchen.

Although the original purpose of writing this book was to preserve many of my mom's great recipes, after several months, an idea came to mind to include recipes from other women whom I have been fortunate to know and consider as my other moms. My mom had met them over the years during her various visits and was thankful for their motherly presence in my life since I live on my own in the United States.

These wonderful ladies, whom I met at different points in my life's journey, have contributed to my well-being, and they, too, were up in their ages. Since I enjoy their dishes as well, I wanted to collect their food recipes to keep as keepsakes.

After successfully pitching this idea to them and gaining their enthusiastic support, the original concept soon evolved into something new and much more profound. I discovered that in addition to sharing our favorite recipes and discussing how our cooking techniques differed from each other, we were soon talking about how the kitchen played an important role in our family's lives.

We were talking about everything, from meaningful communication among family members to knowledge gained from lessons learned.

FROM MY **Mama'sKitchen**®

We were reminiscing about how the kitchen and mealtimes became a wonderful backdrop for, at times, *heavy conversations* between our moms and their children and for discussing family matters.

A *"food for thought"* came to my mind when I realized there was a greater story that needed to be told. If I had stayed with my original intention of collecting and writing only food recipes I like, three of my 9 Moms would not have made it into this heart-centered and passion-driven book project. The reason being, well, what can I say, it is a guy thing; I was on a mission to collect food recipes that I love!

Whether I was divinely guided, the awakened and enlightened me had discovered a treasure trove—a wealth of information that I personally had benefited from over the years and, like most sons and daughters, had taken for granted.

This treasure trove is *"Motherly Love."* It is ageless, universal, transcends cultures, and most importantly, *"It is Unconditional."*

Whether you live in Asia, Europe, Africa, the Middle East, Australia, New Zealand, the South Pacific Islands, or the Americas, all moms have the same desire to share one thing with their children— *to provide food for the soul and recipes for living.* These timeless *"motherly pearls of wisdom"* are shared with all of us in the very first classroom we are enrolled in, *"our home."* Here is where we learn how to successfully navigate our life's journey of learning from the University of Life.

I ended up keeping the same title because it was what started this whole spiritual awakening for me; the From My Mama's Kitchen section highlights kitchen table conversations, which showcase the kitchen as the heart of every home. The Food for the Soul section captures the precious moments of the motherhood journey. The Recipes for Living section provides 30 timeless recipes for living life to complement the various evergreen nuggets of *"motherly wisdom"* sprinkled throughout the other two sections.

Please enjoy reading the upcoming engaging, entertaining, and enlightening pages, and may it help you remember the precious loving moments you have experienced with your mom(s).

We all need **today** to plan for tomorrow. However, we sometimes forget that **today** is actually tomorrow for yesterday.

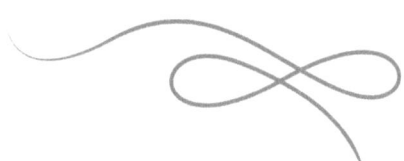

Chapter 1

From My Mama's Kitchen

Although all my moms have different ethnic backgrounds and grew up in different parts of the world and the United States, they all have one thing in common: they all belong to the same generation.

Each one grew up in the late 1920s to the late 1930s and was familiar with less advanced early kitchen devices, which I call the wood-burning stove era. However, what may seem primitive to us today was the technology of their time. Food was cooked three times daily, and everything was prepared from scratch and with fresh ingredients.

Food for Thought: All the food was organically grown and raised. The term shelf life was not in the kitchen dictionary.

Later, depending on economic ability, everyone graduated to using a charcoal stove, then a kerosene stove, and eventually a gas stove.

Regardless of which method they used to cook meals, each was tedious, temperamental, time-consuming, and hazardous.

To further spice up the learning environment, no two days were alike. The weather, supplies, and personal habits or personal behavior tendencies could complicate the cooking process. If the high-maintenance stove was not maintained and cleaned after each use, the neglect was evident the next day when it refused to work properly.

To compound these daily challenges, if one is careless and not paying attention, the lapse in focus could have a disastrous result, from burnt food to a burnt kitchen and even the infliction of injury to oneself.

However, from these daily challenges came a forged character of patience, perseverance, focus, and a totally unique creative thought process that cannot be duplicated outside the kitchen or learned in a formal classroom situation.

Over time, through personal resiliency, a passionate pursuit for personal excellence takes root within oneself. It has been referred to as the character-building period of oneself.

Most of us may not realize this today, and some might even argue about it, but during our grandparents' time and before, the most important asset a woman brought to a marriage was her ability to cook. The kitchen was the most important place in any household because, from there, a family's stability, well-being, and personal wealth could be distinctively measured by the quality of the food cooked and served to the family, relatives, and guests alike.

It was said that if you could conquer the kitchen, then you could do everything else because nothing in life is as challenging or rewarding.

From my various moms' kitchen encounters, I have found that they learned much from their respective mothers. The kitchen became a wonderful classroom for them to learn and be aware of everyday living. They learned to develop self-confidence, how to overcome their personal insecurities while discovering who they were, and ways to refine their unique creative capabilities.

Moving at the steady pace of a marathon, kitchen activities offered plenty of time for meaningful conversations, both external and especially internal, which resulted in effective communications. By contrast, in today's world of microwave cooking and ready-to-eat meals, where everything is a sprint, there is simply not much time to converse anymore.

> **Food for Thought:** *Although we live in an information technology age, where connecting and sharing with others is as easy as pressing a button, we often find ourselves in a "failure to communicate" situation.*

We can all agree that we need to have today in order to plan for tomorrow. In time, we all learn to understand why the past can have so much to offer us in terms of experiences encountered and lessons learned. However, we sometimes forget that today is actually tomorrow for yesterday.

You know you are doing the right thing when your mind is in harmony with your **heart**. The things that make life worth living should always be felt by the **heart** and not purely a thought of the mind.

Chapter 2

It is truly amazing how my life exemplifies the phrase, *"It takes one woman to give birth to a baby, but it takes a village to raise a child"*—in my case, a global village.

Although I was adopted at birth, the love and bonding I received from my parents were not distinguishable from what I saw my friends receive from their birth parents. Being six years younger than my sister, which made me the baby of the family, I was very close to my mom. Dad was pretty much the breadwinner of the family, and mom was the homemaker. She was in charge of the house, and kept my sister and me informed of all family affairs.

Four months after my 18th birthday, I traveled halfway around the world to begin my freshman-year Spring Semester at Louisiana State University in Baton Rouge. My cousin James, who graduated with a Master's degree in Agricultural Engineering from LSU the prior Fall Semester, was instrumental in getting me to the United States to further my studies. I had graduated from Melaka High School, the second oldest school in Malaysia, and was doing pre-university studies to attend one of the local universities when I received a letter from James regarding expanding my educational options. Upon hearing a persuasive encouragement from my late cousin Stanley, James's brother, my parents agreed and supported my decision to take advantage of the opportunity. Although I knew I was up for this exciting new adventure, I could not have imagined what life had in store for me, and so my journey began!

Ever since I can remember, I have always had an active, inquisitive mind, wanting to know the whys and the hows about everything. I want to feel secure about every move I make when deciding my future. I find myself always in the mindset of *"inquiring mind wants to know."*

Ready for Adventure on my First Bicycle

My quest for knowledge and my wanting to know all the answers all the time have led me to many rewarding experiences in the past. Although I had confidence in everything I was doing in life, the very fact that I continually wanted to know the result even before I began had somehow turned the mysteries of life into a guaranteed tale. I did not realize that my passion for excellence was slowly turning into an obsession. I soon realized that what I was actually feeling was not out of confidence, but in all actuality, it was out of insecurity, the fear of failure.

I read somewhere that some of the most successful people are actually some of the most insecure people. Apparently, our embedded insecurities push us to succeed. However, if left unchecked, over time, this drive will shift the equilibrium of success to the opposite side of the scale.

My various moms helped me overcome my insecurities by teaching me not to give the mysteries of life too much thought, as they would eventually gain too much power over me. I shouldn't try to figure out why things are happening the way they are happening but rather roll with the punches and try to get comfortable with a bit of ambiguity, as it is a natural part of life. They taught me it is during these doubtful moments that we find strength within.

I have been fortunate throughout my life to have my various moms appear at the right times to serve as my teachers, coaches, and counselors. They were also the loudest cheerleaders at the various finish lines. The knowledge I have gained from them has helped me to navigate my life successfully over the years through very challenging times.

Here is an interesting take on life... I believe my experience growing up with my mom was probably not that much of a difference from everyone else's experience with their moms. Give or take a few years, from the ages of 10 to 18 years old, we have the *"know-it-all attitude."* Then, from the ages of 19 to 30 years old, we go through a period of maybe we *"didn't-know-it-all attitude."* Eventually, somewhere from the ages of 31 to 40 years old, we finally realized that we *"didn't know anything at all."*

I am reminded of what several of my moms told me in our various conversations, *"You are never an expert in your own backyard."* To me, this phrase is very true indeed, in both our personal and professional lives. The reason is that we are too close to the situation or to the individual, and we become a little complacent in recognizing that this person has, indeed, much to offer us in terms of the solutions and Wisdom we seek.

This happens not because we do not respect the person (a parent, spouse, or business associate); rather, we have a mental block that tells us that we are the leader of those who surround us. We view ourselves as the superior members of the team, so to speak!

We fail to recognize that the truly successful individuals of the world not only learn from everyone they meet but, most importantly, learn their best lessons from their inner circle of contacts.

I have always prided myself on making informed decisions. In order to do this, one has to be mindful of one's decisions because they have consequences, and don't forget you personally own the decisions you made.

Mom always said that everyone sets out to do things right, but sometimes, in the course of doing things right, they may not do the right thing.

Of course, I had to ask my mom, *"How do you know if you are doing the right thing?"* Her answer was quite simple. *"You know you are doing the right thing if your mind is in harmony with your heart."*

In other words, the things that make life worth living should always be felt by the heart and not purely a thought of the mind.

Over the years, I have learned that there are two distinct areas of knowledge we seek as individuals. One is intellectual knowledge, and the other is intellectual wisdom, and both are very different. *Knowledge* is book-smart, whereas *Wisdom* is the application of book-smart knowledge to everyday living.

As children, teenagers, young adults, and even middle-aged people, we often confuse the two. However, as we get older, this soon changes as the age of innocence goes through the rigors and challenges of everyday living.

For lack of a better term, we have just checked ourselves into the reality-of-life hotel, where sometimes nothing is what it seems or, more interestingly, sometimes a situation will change beyond our control.

In his New York Times bestselling book *The 7 Habits of Highly Effective People*, Dr. Stephen Covey puts it best: We have our circle of influence, which is us, and our circle of concern, which is anything that is not us. In a nutshell, we can always manage ourselves, whereas we can only lead others.

Successful people often use the phrase designing one's life in expressing themselves whenever asked, *"How did you do it?"* From my various moms' perspectives, designing one's life is very much like preparing to cook a meal.

Any great chef will tell you that the secret to a delicious dish is not in its cooking but rather in the hours of its preparation. It is during these hours of prepping that the mind lovingly creates the dish and anticipates all the possible scenarios that may pop up unexpectedly during the cooking phase. If, by chance, something unexpected occurs, they are fully prepared to apply their intellectual knowledge to find solutions to go with the flow and still end up with a chef's table of perfect delight.

The true ultimate success in designing one's life actually comes from one's ability to apply the knowledge learned to solve everyday living challenges. In my view, this is where the shortest distance between two points is no longer a straight line but rather an angle. Metaphorically speaking, the term *"angle"* defies the logic of a straight line. This is not actually a math problem but rather a real-life situation; I am not referring to an absolute value or a single-dimensional approach.

Life always provides us with choices that result in consequences. There are no right or wrong choices, but rather lessons to be learned as consequences that prepare us, ironically, for a different set of choices that we will soon encounter if we are granted another day by the grace of God.

After spending time cooking with my mom, I soon realized that the truly delicate part of determining the success of each dish is strictly governed by the degree of detailedness that goes into the prepping of each ingredient. I learned that by rinsing off all seafood with salt water, I can get rid of the slime and the fishy smell prior to cooking, and by mincing and cutting the various fresh condiments/spices to the appropriate sizes, no one particular ingredient will dominate over the other when put together. The result is a simple yet perfectly cooked dish rich in flavor and aroma every time.

I also learned that sometimes, in life, when solving the most difficult challenges, they mirror the challenges of cooking the most delicate dish. Everything has its own time. You cannot rush or cut corners in either one.

In cooking, from start to finish, you have to keep your focus on what is at hand. In living, when facing a challenge, we must not take our eyes off the ball, so to speak.

We sometimes think that we know it all. However, the truth is that the more we think we know, the less we know. Mom had a saying: *"Pay attention. It is only when you are aware of your surroundings and when you give yourself a chance to be in the present moment that you will always learn something new every day."*

In cooking, a slight change in the amount of any ingredient used will result in a different taste for the same dish every time. Furthermore, whenever we use fresh ingredients, the food always tastes better. Mom always said that whenever we are faced with life's challenges, if we use fresh ideas, we will always see a new way to find a resolution.

We all know that marinated meats always taste better than non-marinated ones; likewise, the decision we make after giving it a lot of thought will always be better than a rushed one. Another way of looking at this is what my mom referred to as the lettuce leaves analogy. In any challenging situation, more often than not, there exist layers. All we need is patience, perseverance, and time to peel off the outer layers to reveal the true inner core or root of the challenge.

My mom believes that inherent in every one of us, there is a seed of greatness waiting to be discovered. Therefore, as a mom, it is how you nurture this seed of greatness that will ultimately determine the degree of success in your children and loved ones.

My mom's commitment to excellence for her family is unwavering. She always led by example. We may not realize this; our moms care more about us than we may care about ourselves. This nurturing bond cannot be broken regardless of how challenging the relationship becomes.

> **Food for Thought:** *I remember reading in my high school civics book in Malaysia that DNA only contributes to 30% of our success; the other overwhelming 70% is a result of the environment in which we live.*

Mom taught me that everything is attainable if I am focused, and most importantly, my behavior must match my goal. She puts it best by saying, *"You cannot achieve a full-time reward with a part-time effort."* Whenever the going gets tough, do not lower your expectations; instead, adjust your behavior to meet them. You will always need to have determination, passion, perseverance, humbleness, wisdom, love, and a willing heart to achieve complete success in anything you do.

In understanding the true meaning of **motherly love**, such profound love simply cannot be captured, expressed, and elaborated in any number of written words. It has to be **experienced** and felt by the **heart.**

Chapter 3

My family went through a tremendous change during the 1980s. Dad passed away in March of 1981, a year after I left home to attend college. I was not actually told of his passing until after the funeral service had been completed. I received a letter from home written by my sister on behalf of my mom in the middle of my sophomore Spring Semester exams. My mom made the decision not to burden me with the thought of needing to be home for the funeral. Since my dad had stopped working three years earlier because of his illness, our family's finances had been quite tight. We are a small middle-class family living on family savings, and she figured the money needed to get me home and then back to the United States would be better spent on my educational needs. I can still remember getting up very early one morning before dawn a few days later, deep in emotional trauma, trying to process what had just happened to me and my family. With tears running down my eyes, I ran and ran and ran for miles from my Kirby Smith dormitory to the LSU football stadium, to the track and field stadium, to the baseball stadium, to the student union building, and then all over campus as I was distressed and emotionally overwhelmed.

After my dad's passing, our small family went into survival mode overnight. Through those challenging times, my mom was able to keep cool and maintain her bearings, and she and I practically grew older together through the years, first via letters and then via the phone. I was determined to work hard and create something here in the US where she and I could once again see each other in person. Although it took eight long years, it finally happened. When we last saw each other, I was an 18-year-old teenager; now, I am a young 26-year-old adult. A year and a half earlier, I had bought my first new house in anticipation of our mother-son reunion. I was beyond happy when her long, arduous visa application was finally approved by the immigration office in the US Embassy in Malaysia.

I have always felt that my mom was ahead of her time. Although she will always be somewhat conservative by her generation's standards, her thinking and thought processes have always been progressive. For instance, my mom was the first female in her family to cut her hair to a convenient, practical shoulder length despite the socially acceptable norm of waistline full-length hair. In the 1930s-1940s, a woman's appearance in Malaysia included full-length hair, sarong wraps, and an overall feminine look. Her boldness in cutting her hair to shoulder length allowed her younger sisters to follow suit without repercussions because big sister did it first.

Along with being progressive, her faith has been and will always be a strong suit for her. Mom also serves as the spiritual leader of our family. In many ways, her unrelenting faith that all things will eventually work out for the best has been the enduring force of my success thus far.

We all know that everyday living is challenging by itself, but living every day as a mom is far more difficult than you can imagine, especially when you have to put your best self forward every day, not only for yourself but also for those who are counting on you, your family.

For the most part, a mom's role is essential in any family. Someone is always in need of her time, energy, and attention. However, her role is often misunderstood and underappreciated. While growing up in Malaysia, I thought that my mom picked on me all the time, as it seemed like everything I did was wrong. I misunderstood her unique way of motivation for good, successful behavior tendencies as constant harassment during my years of *"I know it all."*

As I got older, and after being away from home for a long time, I started to understand the true meaning of motherly love. Have I understood it completely? A definite no! The reason is that in the grand scheme of things, such profound love simply cannot be captured, expressed, and elaborated in any number of written words. It has to be experienced and felt by the *heart*.

What is interesting about *motherly love* is that although it is complex and personalized to each individual, it has a common, universal theme: Moms will always be moms. Their passion for wanting their children to succeed in life is the driving force behind their motivation to be good, loving moms.

FROM MY **Mama'sKitchen**®

I remember during my early years, my mom was always there whenever I needed her, and she was always attentive to my needs. Whether it was by nature's design or by her cultural upbringing, she played the role just right. She made sure that my sister and I were always clothed and fed. She never forgot important dates such as birthdays and special events.

Then again, life was quite simple back then in Malaysia. Mom was definitely the head of our household. She pretty much ran our family's operation. If our family was a company, and my dad was the CEO, she was the COO. She made sure we all got up on time daily. Dad was up by 3:30 a.m. every morning to start his workday, and my mom was always up at the same time, preparing his breakfast and seeing him off to work without fail. After taking a short nap, my mom was up and running again at 6:00 a.m., preparing breakfast for my sister and Pele, our family dog.

As for me, I woke up at 6:45 a.m. on weekdays, skipped breakfast, showered, and was on my way to school just in time to make it through the school's front gate before the bell sounded at 7:25 a.m. for the first class to begin.

I cannot ever remember a time when this routine was interrupted because my mom was too sick to fulfill her motherly duties. Like all of us, she got sick from time to time, I am sure; however, she never missed seeing my dad off to work, nor did she miss getting my sister and me off to school.

> ***Food for Thought:*** *Perhaps this is a wonderful moment to reflect on the wedding vow phrase—in sickness and in health.*

My sister and I pretty much got home at about the same time every afternoon, just in time to eat lunch with my mom and dad. This was our family time and an opportunity to converse about the latest happenings of the day. Although it was not as lengthy as our nightly family dinnertime together, it still gave us a chance to unwind and chat about everything. I remember just eating and listening to my mom and dad's conversations, and occasionally, my sister would contribute to the conversation. When I got older, I, too, became involved in this casual family conversation time.

My Sister Leng and Me

I soon learned to work the system. I realized that if I wanted something that perhaps could be labeled as selfish or controversial, I would run it by my sister first and then my mom. Once I got them on my side, I would then bring it up at dinnertime for my dad to OK it, knowing that I already had the full backing of the rest of the family if the request should need a family discussion for final approval.

Soon, food and mealtimes became the backdrop for all of the Tan family's conversations and decision-making times. With this in mind, the kind of food was certainly critical in setting the right mood for the upcoming topic of conversation. My sister and I quickly learned not to upset our mom just before she started to prepare our family meals. Mom's mood would certainly influence the type of dishes we would be eating that night.

I recall an incident between my sister and me in which I continuously picked on her (which is a little brother's duty). This, combined with my sister's continual complaints to our mom about me, caused her to be furious with us. Already having her plate full with her daily chores, our mom ended up being stressed out and feeling flat about our constant sibling squabbling.

In order to teach my sister and me a lesson, she decided not to prepare and cook our family meal with her usual motherly love that day. This resulted in all of us, including our dad, who by now was also furious with my sister and me, having to settle for a boring, bland bowl of soup and rice for dinner.

Besides *motherly love*, if there is another common theme that exists among all families in every culture of the world, it is that if our mom is unhappy or upset, the whole family is in the *doghouse*.

On the other hand, you will be surprised by the positive energy that good and delicious dishes can create when you need that extra *Chi* (energy) to be with you. Trust me on this! Good food translates to happy feelings, which then leads to a good mood and attitude, and you know the rest of the story...

Mealtime also contributed to my family's learning about our present and long-lost relatives, as well as our family tree. It was during these times that our family genealogy was passed on from generation to generation through storytelling. Believe me; whether it was over-exaggerated or not, an auntie's sinful act of running off with so-and-so, breaking a family tradition, or the adventurous exploits of a cousin with his carefree attitude about life, all were covered during the 45 minutes to an hour of dinnertime.

Soon, my sister and I were so caught up in and fascinated with the various real-life stories that we were actually now more interested in what the topic of conversation would be rather than what we were going to chow down on. Due to the stories and topics discussed, some of our best mealtime conversations occurred when we had guests at the dinner table.

Interestingly enough, family mealtime experiences were not exclusive to the Tan family, which I discovered through my conversations with my various moms. They all had the same experiences growing up in their respective families and cultures. Although we may be separated by land and water, when it comes to the human factor, we all have the same tendencies and experiences, perhaps in different generations, but nonetheless the same.

It is apparent that mealtimes were the center of our family time because they were an opportunity for everyone to chat, converse, and share the latest happenings. My various moms and I were all able to reflect back on the funny-fun times, the humor, the dramas, and the little private sacrifices our moms made for us and our families that somehow went unnoticed by us as children at that time.

Like an iceberg, only a third is visible; the other two-thirds are under the surface of the water. In our shortsightedness and complacency, we usually do not realize that the complete package is more than what meets the eye.

When we were children, we tended to focus on what was wrong with our moms; that is, she did not support me in this or that. Although some of these had merit, we only saw what we wanted to see and remember. However, through our mom's eyes, we are perfect, flaws and all. She will even come up with reasoning to help justify our shortcomings.

From my own enlightenment and experiences shared by my various moms, I can assure you of this: we can never love our mom more than she loves us. Although some moms may not know how to express their true *motherly love* in the way we expect or anticipate, do not let this fool us. She will always be more excited to see us than we are to see her, and she will always be more proud of us than we can ever be of ourselves.

Johnny Tan

In putting together this book, all of my moms and I agreed that we could always bridge all generations with a little mindfulness and unconditional love by having a genuine appreciation of our own mothers—*the forgotten heroes in our lives.*

Being a mom is like being in
the kitchen: It is all about
creating and loving. It requires
patience, a happy attitude,
and a touch of love.

Chapter 4

I often refer to my life as a pot of Gumbo that is continuously on the simmer, slowly cooking to perfection. Like the famous, delicious Louisiana Gumbo, I, too, have many ingredients in my pot—a dash of this, a smidgen of that, and a pinch of something uniquely special from all my moms I have known over the years.

Amazingly, whenever I needed the right spice to give my Gumbo the right flavor, I could be certain that I could reach into my condiment cupboard and find the right one. Like a professional chef who always has his or her collection of secret ingredients and spices, I have been fortunate to have my own private collection of moms who possess just the right ingredients to help me decode my life's journey and make sense of the various challenges that life throws my way.

These women have been wonderful teachers, coaches, counselors, and cheerleaders for me, as they all share the common inspiring and empowering leadership quality of *motherly love*.

What is motherly love? It's personal sacrifice, it's encouragement, and it's the activity in the kitchen that supplies loving nourishment for the family. Motherly love is that special love that embraces maternal instincts, bonding all moms to their children in every corner of the world.

I have heard others describe motherly love based on their own experiences with their moms, and it is interesting to hear the different descriptions from these various individuals. It is from these entertaining and powerful descriptive stories that I have learned how "*Our Past Always Helped Shape the Present and Inspires the Future!*"

For example, for those of you who are into hard rock bands of the 70s and 80s, Gene Simmons of the Rock & Roll Hall of Famer band KISS once said on an Entertainment TV show interview, "*When I was a kid, my mom used to tell me that she would throw herself under the bus to save me. I did not understand it then, but now, as a father, I understand what she said then.*"

My Southern Belle mom, Eleanora, was the very first mom I met when I arrived in the United States in January 1980. She and her wonderful husband, Nick Carter, were volunteer host families for foreign students at Louisiana State University in Baton Rouge for many years. They were actually the host family for my cousin James and his family for the previous couple of years. Upon completing his Master's in Agricultural Engineering, James returned home to Malaysia with his family just three weeks prior to my arrival in Baton Rouge. I had only been in the United States for three days when Eleanora and Nick graciously invited me over for dinner. They helped me acclimate to the winter weather and acquainted me with living in Baton Rouge.

Born and raised in New Orleans, Louisiana, and graduated from Newcomb College, Eleanora was a natural at being prim, proper, and polished at all times. Her personal elegance and refinement were evident in all areas of her life, including the manner in which she kept up with her extensive doll collection. Her happy demeanor and nurturing nature made it difficult not to give in or agree with her whenever she had her mind set on doing something and accomplishing a task. Whether she had it all planned out as a strategy or not, I was soon eating "Sunday Dinners" with her and Nick just about every weekend. She was the only mom who was able to make me eat my veggies and like them. And, no, I do not eat vegetables!

I remember once, while I was in her kitchen helping her with our big Easter dinner, she eloquently described to me that being a mom is like being in the kitchen: *it is all about creating and loving.* When you are in the kitchen, you are creating something special. It requires patience, a happy attitude, and a touch of love. It is the blending and manifestation of these three primary ingredients that ultimately produce a signature dish.

When food is prepared with love, it always tastes so much better. When life's challenges are approached with the same attitude, even the toughest of the tough will eventually soften.

Although we all may eat the same food, including chicken, fish, pork, beef, or vegetables, we can blend different spices when cooking them to get different flavors. Likewise, applying a different approach to the same challenge will give us a different outcome every time.

In understanding *"food for the soul,"* as described in the upcoming chapters, we need to recognize several traits our moms have that are unique and special. All of my moms told me the same thing: that no one can be totally prepared for motherhood. Yes, you can read about it, you can hear someone else talk to you about it, and you can even briefly babysit or take care of your godchild or a relative's child; however, the end experience, the connection, is never the same until you have one you can call your very own, either by birth or by adoption.

Then you are committed for life, 24 hours a day, seven days a week, and it is never-ending. In an instant, you are thrust into a new sense of responsibility, a new sense of acute awareness of everything that is happening around you, and you will soon develop skills you never knew you had.

You are now a psychic, a romance guru, a quartermaster, a family banker, a spiritual leader, a family doctor, a motivator and educator, and a visionary who envisions success in your child long before he or she can even call out your name.

No matter how much formal education we have, no matter how much material wealth we have accumulated, our mom will always have tasted more salt of life than we have. In short, ***living wisdom***.

Chapter 5
Food for The Soul

Mom is a Psychic—She has all-seeing-eyes and peripheral vision. "I am watching you," she says. She is able to see the future. She has bionic ears and is a human lie detector.

Our moms have natural instincts to watch us as babies just about all of the time, although some do it better than others. They read us like a book. The sounds we make, our body language, our demeanor, and the tone and pattern of our voice are all noted and stored permanently in their memory bank.

All of these skills are developed to ensure our safety, security, and happiness at all times. However, these motherly behavior skills soon evolve into what I refer to as *motherly psychic ability*.

Call it a mother's intuition if you like, but this ability is honed to perfection over time. From our end, as children, we sometimes feel that our moms have eyes on the back of their heads, or perhaps they have a crystal ball hidden somewhere. They can see right through us. They can tell if we are happy, sad, troubled, or outright lying.

My mom's favorite line always begins with "I see you are…" When I hear her say this, if I am ready to seek her counsel and talk about it, I will take that opening line as a loving and comforting remark and dive into opening up my innermost troubled feelings.

However, if I am not quite ready to talk about it, especially when I know the feedback I am going to get is not what I want to hear just yet, I will retreat into the fail-safe mode of *self-denial*.

Mom has a saying she uses on me all the time. "No matter how much formal education you have, no matter how much material wealth you have accumulated, I will always have tasted more salt of life than you have." In short, *living wisdom*.

In one of the many conversations I had with my Cajun mom, Ginger, she told me this about one of her sons. *"I know there is something bothering him, but he is not ready to talk about it yet. He does not think I am aware that he is troubled, but I can detect it in his voice. Mama will always be ready whenever he is ready to open up."*

Ginger and I met at one of the weekly ballroom dance parties hosted by Rick Seeling Dance Studio in Baton Rouge, Louisiana, in the fall of 2000. A honeybee farmer by day and a beginner ballroom dancer by night, she was a little timid in getting onto the dance floor to dance. After convincing her that I, too, was a newbie and that "the blind will be leading the blind," she cracked up, grabbed my hand, and led me to the dance floor to dance the jitterbug. She had seen me dance before and knew that I could dance; she was delighted that I took the time to put her mind and nerves at ease. For that, she could not let the opportunity to dance slip away without giving it a try.

From that day onward, we became good friends. Besides her Cajun fried turkey and her alligator sauce piquante, Ginger's practical approach to life and her jovial personality are just the right prescription at times in spicing and jazzing up my daily routine a little bit whenever I needed a little dose of humor to uplift my confidence. Her favorite phrase for me is "And the Good News is…" As an invited contributor to the Chicken Soup for the Soul bestselling book series since 2015, it was a delight to share my heart-centered fourth story about Ginger and her, "And The Good News Is…" which was featured in the chapter titled Always There for Us, in their 2019 Chicken Soup for the Soul: Mom Knows Best collection.

Mom is a Romance Guru—When it comes to romance, mom can see it coming from a mile away—the good, the bad, and the ugly. What she is saying is that she can give us an accurate analysis printout, so to speak, of any behavioral tendencies in our potential mate that may have a long-term impact on our relationship.

It is by nature that our mom wants the best for us. The best is a person who will love us and take care of us as well as she does. In all actuality, she is looking for her replacement. She wants to make sure that we are not blinded by the heat of the moment or we don't fail to see, in some instances, the hairline fractures that, when left unattended, can develop into a major fault line one day, which can threaten the wellness of the relationship.

My mom has a theory about courtship. "It is true you are not the only bee flying around out there; however, she is certainly not the only flower in the garden either. Her loss is someone else's gain!"

Mom's concept of everlasting love is quite impressive, too. Although she believes no one is perfect, she also believes in some basic fundamental parameters. Like cooking, there simply must be some *must-have* key ingredients to enable love to grow between two individuals that will ultimately sustain the, at times, bumpy rides of the relationship.

These ingredients may look simple and appealing by themselves, depending on the day's flavor. However, when combined, they yield a potent, sustaining compound called *everlasting love*.

No one ingredient outweighs the other in importance, nor can there be a failing grade in any one of them. The key is to achieve and maintain a passing grade in all ingredients every day in every way. How does one do it? All my moms have the same answer: we simply make the right loving choices every day of our lives.

According to my various moms, one of the choices they make in a loving relationship is to express their love through verbal and nonverbal communication. Many times, the nonverbal communications actually speak louder than the verbal ones.

Quite simply put, in order for a good, loving soul mate relationship to experience a sustaining success, it must have the following basic ingredients: spiritual connection, emotional connection, intellectual connection, communicational connection, and physical connection.

Spiritual Connection—Both need to be spiritually grounded, believing that there is an unseen power that is greater than both in this universe. The families that pray and worship together are more likely to stay together.

Emotional Connection—Both need to have empathy for the other's needs. Both need to be responsible and take ownership of themselves. Be in an interdependent relationship rather than a codependent relationship.

Intellectual Connection—Both need to agree on the concept of *ours or oneness versus mine and yours*. The needs of the family as a whole always outweigh the needs of any individual. Having a mutual understanding of the difference between a want and a need is the key to achieving success in this area.

Communicational Connection—Both need to have the ability to talk about anything, and everything, with the emphasis on listening to learn rather than listening in anticipation to reply.

Physical Connection—Both need to respect the law of physical attraction. It should not fade away with having a family, nor should it fade away with age. The secret to the everlasting desire for each other is in the ongoing creation of intimate moments by our own design.

I first met my 91-year-old foster Italian mom, Carol, in the summer of 1980 when I accepted her husband, Ben Wisdom's invitation to visit them in Poplar Bluff, Missouri. Perhaps faith was already in the works for me because while transiting in Seoul, South Korea, on my way to the United States, I met Ben. He is a mild-mannered midwestern gentleman and a World War II veteran who was returning from a business trip to Asia with his business partner. He invited me to visit and stay with family in between semesters that summer.

Carol instantly took a liking for me, and by the end of the three-week stay in Poplar Bluff, which, by the way, is a beautiful, homey city that lies along an escarpment separating the foothills of the Ozarks, she invited me to be a part of her family, and I found myself having a foster family.

Later that fall, Ben rerouted his Asia business trip schedule to visit my family in Melaka, Malaysia. He wanted to let my parents know that he and Carol are happy to step in as surrogate parents whenever I need assistance in the U.S. They have embraced me as a member of their family, assuring my parents that everything will be safe from a parenting perspective. Little did I know Ben's presence in my life was God-sent. He visited my family six months after my father's passing to ensure my mom and sister that I would be looked after accordingly and also updated me with the latest news from home.

Over the years, besides breaking bread with the Wisdom family during the Christmas holiday season and enjoying Carol's homemade Muffulettas, Italian sausage, Chicken and Dumplings, and Pecan Coconut pie, I also benefited from her insightful advice on my personal life and daily challenges when I found myself in those situations and needed to talk them out.

She once emailed me a wonderful article she described as *something to think about*. The timing of her email was perfect, as I was going through a period in my life when I needed a better understanding when it comes to love and relationships. This article apparently has been floating around in cyberspace for a while. The author is unknown; however, the insightful meaning reaches deep into the very essence of what it is really all about in making the right choice in our personal lives.

Johnny Tan

I would like to share this wonderful article, "*Is it a Choice or a Chance?*" with you. I hope that you will get as much out of it as I did when I first read it.

Is it a Choice or a Chance?
(Author unknown)

When you meet the right person to love, you are at the right place at the right time.
That is a chance.

When you meet someone you are attracted to, that is not a choice.
That is a chance.

Being caught up in the moment
(and there are many couples who get together like this) is not a choice
That is also a chance.

The difference is what happens afterward.
When will you take that infatuation,
that crush, that mind-blowing attraction to the next level?

This is when sanity kicks in;
you sit down and contemplate on whether you want to make this into a concrete relationship or just a fling.

If you decide to love a person, even with his/her faults,
that is not a chance.
That is a choice.

When you choose to be with a person, no matter what,
that is a choice.

Although you know there are many people out there

*who are more attractive, smarter, and richer
than your mate is, and yet you decide to love your mate just the same,
that is a choice.*

*Infatuations, crushes, and attractions come to us by chance.
However, true love that lasts is truly a choice,
a choice that we make.*

*Regarding soul mates, there is a beautiful movie quote,
which I believe is so true:
"Fate brings you together,
but it's still up to you to make it happen."*

*I believe soul mates do exist,
that there is truly someone created for everyone.
However, it is still up to us to make the choice
if we are going to do something about it or not.*

*We may meet our soul mate by chance,
but loving and staying with our
soul mate is still a choice we have to make.*

*Our challenge in this world is not finding someone perfect to love,
but rather to learn how to love an imperfect person perfectly!*

*...have Faith, have Hope, and most importantly—
have the greatest of all—
have Love.*

Mom is a Quartermaster—She is a procurement expert. The family's interest always comes first, ahead of hers. Whether you need something or request something you need, she will ultimately be the judge of whether your request is a need or a want. Rest assured that your needs will always be met almost immediately, as your justification becomes her justification. I can reflect back on many situations and instances when my mom came through for me on just about anything I asked for, simply because that was all I needed to do.

This brings us to Mom being the family's private banker. I am not talking about her having a Swiss Bank account that nobody knows about; rather, it is a Mama's Piggy Bank, an emergency fund put away somewhere safe for unexpected rainy days. My mom always preached to my sister and me, *"It is the savings you do during the good times that matters most, rather than the spending you do during the times of plenty."*

My late Sanguine Savannah mom, Toni, whom I met in October of 1985 while I was at a business function in the beautiful city of Savannah, Georgia, described it best. *"Live like there is no tomorrow; however, always plan that you will have another day to live."*

Have you ever felt that once in a while in our life, we encounter people who somehow make us feel like we have known each other for years? Toni and I felt that way about each other when we first met. She and I kept in touch over the years, and having a son who is a few years older than me gave her a greater understanding of the current and latest plights I went through, generationally speaking. Always warm and nurturing, her wise insights and carefree, positive outlook on life facilitated her being a great encourager whenever I needed a cheerleading moment.

Amazingly, all of my moms have a secret fund for unexpected rainy days! Looking back in time, we all know now that, as children, we never wanted anything; we always needed everything. Therefore, this contingency fund was always in use in my family.

Mom is the family's Spiritual Leader—She is the spiritual guide for the family. Ever since I can remember, I recall my mom bringing my sister and me to the various temples on holy days to pray to God for his blessings and guidance in our daily lives and to renew the right spirit in us every day in every way. She personally prayed for the family twice a day, at sunrise and at sunset.

She told my sister and me a long time ago, *"Always remember this—it doesn't matter what religious affiliation you belong to or practice, the most important thing to remember is that you have to believe that there is a greater force and power that exists other than all of us, called GOD, who orchestrates the laws of the universe. There will be times, situations, and occurrences that cannot be explained when all logic goes out the window, and faith steps in to save the day—this is Spiritual Grounding."*

Mom is the family's Doctor—She always has a treatment for everything. At times, she will even have a family-handed-down secret remedy that is almost a cure-all. Sometimes, it is just the mere loving attention you get that does the trick. I have learned over the years that *motherly love* can sometimes be the only *panacea* you need whenever you are sick or feeling blue.

I once had a conversation with a father about how he learned of the power of motherly love from his ten-year-old son. The boy was not feeling well and needed something to eat, so since his wife was still at work, he decided to cook his son's favorite noodle soup.

Feeling proud about what he had done for his son, he said to him, "Here you are; I have cooked your favorite noodle soup for you, just like mommy does." His son responded by thanking him but also added, "When mommy cooks hers, she always cooks it with love."

Needless to say, his son's comment blew him away because he realized that it was true. The only reason he had cooked the meal was that it was simple. Had it been a different dish that his son wanted to eat, he would have had to wait for his mom to get home from work.

> ***Food for Thought:*** *I guess we all know now that it is not the chicken soup that did the trick, but rather the motherly love that went into the cooking of the soup that did it!*

My Mom, Sister, and Me (2007)

Mom is the family's Motivator and Educator—My mom grew up during a time and generation that did not provide her with the opportunity for a formal education. However, she knew what the value of a good, quality education could do for her children's futures.

Although she did not know how to read or write, she knew what the letters A, B, C, D, and F looked like and what each represented in the field of academia. Notice that the letter E is not important to her as it is irrelevant to her motherly mission. She also knew the color codes used in the Malaysian educational system at the time to express the merit of the grade awarded for good academic work—the color blue represented a passing grade, and the color red represented a failing grade.

Therefore, my sister and I could not bluff our way out of receiving any bad grades. Mom also knew when to expect our quarterly report cards. She had it marked on her "special calendar" and was always ready to dish out the appropriate persuasive punishments for the less-than-desired grades earned by my sister and me.

In spite of being the toughest teacher my sister and I had, our mom was also the greatest motivator for us. She continuously kept us focused on education by providing us with all the necessary tools for success. We got everything we asked for when it was school-related.

With just the right amount of discipline and parental guidance, she always made my sister, and I understand one thing. "*I, as your mother, have done everything I can to help you succeed in school; however, if you do not, then it must have been fated that way.*"

After hearing that speech several times, if my sister and I were still sputtering along, my mom always came up with another trick to get us motivated because, in her eyes, failure was not an option!

Mom is a Visionary—She believes in faith and expectancy and always looks for the best in us. She always looks beyond the surface and straight into the heart. Mom always believes that it is the attitude of our hearts that ultimately defines us.

During the early years of my life in the United States, when doubts tried to take center stage, I always found my internal strength by reflecting on the tremendous sacrifice my mom made and the determination she had to send me halfway around the world.

Over the years, her unwavering strength and conviction in mastering the power of faith and divine destiny within herself have served as a beacon of hope and a renewed right spirit and passion for me whenever I am in need of a little refresher in my purpose-driven life.

From an early age, my mom always knew how to enlarge her circle of knowledge and expand beyond the boundaries of her comfort zone. She knew our life experiences always govern our behavior. She always taught me to dream about the future and engage in all possibilities with hope.

Mom always believed that I could do anything and that I was capable of accomplishing everything. She may not verbalize her proud feelings, but I can see them in her eyes, actions, and intentions.

She has an interesting way of getting her point across by telling me that solving the most difficult challenges can mirror the challenge of cooking the most delicate dish. Everything has its own time, and we cannot rush or cut corners for either one.

Over the years, I have realized that no matter what challenges I am currently facing, my mom knows what to say and how to say it to make me feel better. Mom is always there as a teacher, a coach, a counselor, and a cheerleader for me.

Throughout our life's journey, we will continue to gain and encounter new experiences. Some experiences, good or bad, will stay with us for the rest of our lives. It is **how we manage them** that will ultimately determine our idea of success or failure in both our personal and professional lives.

Chapter 6

As we evolve through the various stages of our lives, from baby to teenager to young adult to adulthood, our moms move along with us through different phases of their *motherly love*.

According to my various moms, if not at conception, then certainly during delivery, moms, in just an instant, realize that their lives have just changed forever. The most important person in their lives is no longer themselves; rather, it is us. From that day forward, consciously and subconsciously, they are on a personal mission for the next 18 or more years to be the best teachers they can be for us.

In their minds, they know we do not know anything about anything, and it is their responsibility to educate us on everything they know to prepare us for life. My mom used to tell me, "*I am certain I am not going to outlive you, so I have to make sure when I am gone, you are well taken care of and that I have done everything I could to ensure just that.*"

Although there may be rare exceptions to this, from the day we are born, our moms take total responsibility and ownership of taking care of us. They will continue to do this for the rest of their lives, standing strong and unwavering in their love for us. Whether by natural or acquired leadership skills, they have the ability to relate the ABCs of life and living to us as children.

We may not realize this, but with their unconditional support and love, they are always proud of us. In their eyes, we are never wrong; we just make mistakes. There are lessons to be learned, and we are taught by experiencing them as we navigate through life in order to live our perfect lives in an imperfect world.

However, somewhere during the second half of this 18-year span, when we hit puberty and became teenagers, we somehow find *enlightenment.* In our own personal way, we are convinced that *"we know it all"* about life and living and that mom, in our minds, is just being cynical and overprotective, as she herself doesn't know everything and perhaps nothing at all. When we are young adults between the ages of 19 and 30, we eagerly leave home to be on our own and enroll full-time in the University of Life to pursue a career or higher education. We soon discover that we may not know as much as we thought we did.

On the other hand, our mom, feeling fresh with the sense of elation that we are now out of the house and, on our own, gently moves toward the coaching phase of their motherly love. Having raised us all these years, they are able to identify our abilities and our hidden talents because they know our upper and lower limits in handling everyday challenges.

With this in mind, they know just what to do or say, using different approaches to help us navigate through and understand life's lessons. However, our level of maturity and sense of responsibility play a key role in determining whether she will move from a teacher to a coach and how quickly this will occur.

The coaching phase will definitely become more prominent as the months and years go by. Our very own sense of independence and our *"we-know-it-all"* attitude as we are eager to be the *man or woman* we aspire to be will further fuel this transition process.

Sensing this, our moms eagerly accommodate us because they know we need the experience of living on our own in order for us to recognize and truly appreciate them and their motherly love for us.

In all actuality, our actions draw out the coaching skills of our moms. How do we do this, you ask? Well, as young adults, we let our pride get in our way just about all the time.

Driven by the *"I-know-it-all"* mentality, we are always on guard. We will do or go as far as we can with just about any challenging situation, and even talk it over with other people besides our mom because we do not want our mom to know that we may not *"know it all"* after all.

On the other hand, like seasoned coaches, our moms can sense our situation and *"the pride thing"* within us. Therefore, they use different approaches with us so that they do not come across with the *"I-told-you-so"* attitude.

They can see this in us from afar because they read us like a book. Remember, they have been studying us for all these years, and they have us memorized. They realize that if they approach us right, they won't bruise our ego and may actually come across as our best friend. In some instances, they do become our *"new wise best friend"* in the process. For some of us, we are fortunate to experience this sooner rather than later in life.

Over time, as we encounter a series of events, experiences, and real-life situations, we soon realize that we have actually retained some very valuable insights that our moms had taught us during our *"know-it-all"* years.

This realization transitions us into the counseling phase of motherly love. Some of us reach this point at 31 years old, give or take a few years, while others may wander in the wilderness for a few more decades before realizing that we *"do not know it all,"* or worse still, we become too proud to admit that we do not know it all.

However, as for our mom, she is always all ears. She has the ability to listen effectively and understand completely what we are going through in life. Although she feels helpless at times for not being able to wave her magic wand to fix everything or make everything better, she always has words of encouragement, advice, and wisdom to share with us at any given moment.

Realizing our strengths and weaknesses and knowing our personal upper and lower limits, she will offer us *"windows of solutions"* to choose from, best fitting our desired outcomes. She knows from her own personal experiences that whenever someone is in a crisis mode or a difficult situation, he or she has a *"tunnel vision."* By sharing with us the various possible options, she is leading us to choose and take the right course of action in order for us to achieve optimum success while operating well within our own comfort zones.

Mom always talked about knowing thyself or self-awareness. This is very important because who we are *"today"* is a sum of who we were yesterday. This is not just in the physical sense but also, most importantly, from a psychological, spiritual, and emotional sense.

I remember my mom telling me just before I left home to go to college in the United States, *"Your dad and I have done the best we know how in raising you and have loved you to the best of our abilities. Since childhood, you have been exposed to all kinds of experiences, and now you are about to embark on your life's journey, where you will continue to gain and encounter new experiences. Some experiences, good or bad, will stay with you for the rest of your life. However, it is how you manage them that will ultimately determine your idea of success or failure in both your personal and professional life."*

Throughout my life, I have always found myself in a leadership position. I am a natural at taking charge whenever there is a need and when no one else steps up. Whether I am driven by passion or obsession, I always manage to get things done successfully by leading people and managing situations.

My Sanguine Savannah mom, Toni, once told me about the difference between obsession-driven living and passion-driven living. We would get the same result of having things right and perfect every time with both; however, obsession is mentally driven, whereas passion is heart-driven.

My Progressive and Spiritual mom, Elsa Mae, and I have known each other since the spring of 1987 when we were introduced to each other by a mutual friend, Fern Hyde, at one of her parties in Hammond, Louisiana. Although having been retired for a number of years at that time, Elsa Mae always found time to be involved in activities where her people skills were in great demand. Her greatest assets are her ability to see beyond what meets the eye and to articulate with confidence in any setting without compromising her beliefs and principles, all with a touch of spiritual wisdom.

Often labeled as a people person myself, I connected with Elsa Mae instantly. She has the aura of a sweet Southern lady everyone would like to have as a grandma—always full of smiles and love. One of the fondest memories I have of Elsa Mae is that even when she was 90 years old, she never forgot to make that one call every year. She is the only mom who calls me at midnight (actually at 12.01 a.m.) on my birthday to wish me "Happy Birthday."

In one of her many pieces of advice to me, Elsa Mae said, *"In a real-life situation, happiness is always felt by the heart rather than thought of by the mind."* Although we can choose to be happy, ultimately, we still need to feel happy.

What is true about this is that when we are obsessed with something, someone, or a situation, we tend to develop a narrow vision. Not only do we have our blinders on, but we are now in self-fulfilling mode, and most of the time, we have a total disregard for the human factor. We operate based on "me" instead of "us" and, thus, pursue everything as a solo act with one goal in mind—winning at all costs.

Johnny Tan

Dianne, Elsa Mae, and My Mom Nyah

On the other hand, with a heartfelt, passionate approach towards everything in life, we take the human factor into the equation. Just by doing this, the energy of collaborative partnership will, in turn, create individual ownership of a shared vision.

How do we create a passion for everything we do? Betty, my Ballroom Dance Instructor mom, advised me to do a reality check. I met Betty in 1996 through two mutual friends, Vickie Liard and Sandy Schmidt, who were, at that time, on a mission to recruit young men into their ballroom dancing group. Vickie was a lovely lady who worked for the Baton Rouge Area Convention and Visitors Bureau, where I was one of their board directors. I seemed to fit their profile quite nicely— young, single, and with time to spare. Believe it or not—as it was back then, as it is today—men who can dance and lead women on the dance floor are always hot commodities in the ballroom dancing world.

Betty taught ballroom dancing for over 30 years and had a loyal following of students who literally had been with her for just about as long as she had been in the business. She grew up in the Midwest and played professional women's basketball for a short period of time before joining the Arthur Murray Dance Studio as a dance instructor. She later left to start her own dance studio.

I can still recall the first question she asked me when we met: *"Do you want to dance, or do you want to DANCE?"* This question became the foundation of my ballroom dancing and confidence education. Knowing very little about dancing, I replied, "What is the difference?" Boy, did I open the floodgates that would sweep me away into a new journey of life's lessons!

With a smile, Betty replied, *"If you want to dance, I will teach you some dance patterns that you can apply easily to the different music."* As she moved around the dance floor, showing me some dance moves. She added, *"However, if you want to DANCE!, I will teach you this."* She gracefully raised her arms, stretched upwards and outwards with a soft left-side poised Waltz position.

Having been infected by the WOW factor, without much thought, I excitedly answered, *"Yes, I want to learn the Waltz, just like that, the way you showed me!"* In my mind, I am 35; four weeks earlier, I had just earned my black belt in the Korean martial arts, Tang Soo Do; how difficult can this be? Betty was thrilled with my decision, and we started on my dancing journey.

Well, I spoke too soon; three weeks into my new adventure, I had to go to the Gym three times a week and work on muscles I didn't know existed to keep up with the 66-year-old lady. Within weeks, she whipped me into shape and taught me rhythm, integrating my heart, mind, body, and spirit to work together in concert, to glide and flow on the dance floor effortlessly. Betty helped me tap into the rhythmic essence I already possessed but was dormant, just waiting for the right time to come out to play and express myself!

It was during this time that Betty and I soon realized that we share many common interests in community wellness and similar goals for our personal growth—a passion for excellence in everything we do.

She got me to start taking a personal inventory of myself—my strengths, my weaknesses, my likes, my dislikes, what I can tolerate, what I cannot tolerate, and what is important and not important in my life.

For the first time, I started opening my third eye, which is my consciousness. I really paid attention to what was around me, and then I realized that the answers were all around me. From people to situations, there were signs everywhere. I then realized that extremes on either end of the spectrum were not good. The middle was where I needed and wanted to be, balanced and prioritized.

While heavily immersed in my career at that time, I realized that I was consumed by the rush of achieving success after success. However, I also started to notice others who did not move at the same pace and were actually content with their lives. These individuals represented one side of the spectrum in their own sublime happiness from their perspective, and the other side represented me, those who moved too fast to enjoy life.

In introspection, this balance was not a new phenomenon. I could vividly recall how happy I was growing up during the age of innocence, being involved in many different sporting activities. I was always good at everything I decided to focus on; however, I was never obsessed with any particular sport. I have always had the attitude of wanting to do respectably in anything I choose to participate in. I was and still am very competitive but not obsessive.

My competitiveness comes from a predetermination of the game and my opponent. I can still recall not diving for a ball and risking injury on myself in a game of tennis or racquetball because I was confident I would win the point lost in the subsequent serve. If my opponent won, he deserved the victory for the day. I just needed to regroup and train harder for a rematch on another day.

Also, during this time of reflection, I had just finished reading Dr. Stephen Covey's *The 7 Habits of Highly Effective People*. The book discusses writing down a personal vision and mission statement in order to make a personal paradigm shift in one's life. In preparing myself to do this, I recalled the various advice, anecdotes, and insights I had received from my various moms regarding how to live my life, how I want to be remembered, and what I want to contribute to the community in which I live.

Writing my personal vision and mission statements was the toughest thing I had to do. The reason is that from that moment onwards, I have a personal road map for the rest of my life. This declared who I am, and since it was on paper, it became a personal contract with myself. From then on, what I do defines me.

Since then, a big part of my daily life has been living each day in *"today."* My Texan Earthly mom, Dee, always said that although we are here today, we tend to live our lives in *"yesterday or tomorrow."* We let the worries of yesterday affect how we feel today, or we let our minds wander off to planning for tomorrow. When we do this, we simply forget to enjoy the wonders of today and are not living our lives in the moment.

Dee and I met in 1986 when I engaged the services of her employment agency to help me recruit managers for the company I was working for at that time. After spending much professional time together, we soon became close friends. Her business sense and pragmatic motherly advice over the years have been instrumental in giving me valuable, unique insights on how I can apply fresh new perspectives in dealing with life's daily challenges.

One piece of her advice that I will always keep close to heart is, *"If we use yesterday as a point of reference rather than a guide, we can certainly enjoy planning for tomorrow, today. However, if we use yesterday as a guide, then tomorrow and today will always be the same as they were yesterday."*

I have since learned to live my life in the moment and have faith in everything I do. It was not easy in the beginning, but over a period of several months, I started to see the fruits of what was greater than I could imagine. I soon discovered that instead of feeling stressed and mentally exhausted, I had better control in all areas of my life.

This new control was not out of my subconscious fear and insecurities but rather came from a position of cognitive power of reasoning. Although the rational side of my brain wanted to take control, my emotional heart always managed to step up to the plate and maintain a good balance in everything I did.

This newfound understanding also gave me the peace and quiet confidence to leave a very successful 18-year career with a major company in the restaurant industry, the last seven years as its Chief Operating Officer, to pursue a lifelong dream of owning my own business.

Sometimes, I catch myself worrying about yesterday or planning for tomorrow. When this happens, I quickly remind myself to stay in the present moment by counting my blessings and thanking God for the gifts I have for today.

Over the years, I encountered many personal and professional challenges that had certainly pushed me to the extreme limits. It was during these challenging times that I discovered how strong the foundation of my spiritual DNA is. I knew then if I had not given up *control* of my life and started believing in *faith* and *destiny*, I would have easily folded and lost hope in all areas of my life.

It is all in our *"attitude."* If we treasure every moment, then every day is a *"Gift."* When my dear friend and dance partner Carrie suddenly and tragically passed on, I learned that nothing is permanent and that people, life, and moments are all *"one,"* in the same sense that *"yesterday is history, tomorrow may not come, and all I have is today."*

I am thankful to God for another occasion for giving me the opportunity to spend the last hours with my late Ballroom Dancing Instructor mom, Betty, who had somehow hung on for me to be there with her before she passed on. The experience reminded me of the simple yet special things in life to be grateful for, and the wisdom of today is not to miss any opportunity to make a positive difference in someone's life.

I now use my heart to guide and lead me in all my decision-making processes, and I use my rational mind to find solutions for whatever challenges I encounter along the way. I find that I have gained a true balance in all areas of my life. I am now able to combine my intellectual knowledge with how I truly feel in my heart, giving me the peaceful and quiet confidence to make a well-balanced and informed decision at all times. I am happy and successful inside and out.

Betty, Carrie. and Me

As we mature, our relationships with our moms mature too, as no one particular role is more important than the other; only the situation at hand will dictate the role required to address the specific issue in life.

At the same time, not all moms are experts in all the roles, either. Some are stronger in one, two, or even three of these areas. I have been fortunate that the various moms in my life over the years have met my various needs when I needed answers to my questions.

As we understand and accept that we are not perfect ourselves, neither are our moms; however, their love for us is genuine. They will always love us the best way they know how and will be ready to impart their living wisdom to us through their various *recipes for living*.

All great recipes survive through the generations. Although some may be modified and refined to keep pace with the flavor and taste buds of today, they will continue to be handed down to **future generations** in each family.

Chapter 7
Recipes for Living

If you love cooking and enjoy the process, this should come as no surprise, as it is common to encounter demanding and complicated recipes when cooking great meals. No matter how challenging or complex the recipe was, my mom always started with the end in mind. She knew the exact flavor, texture, and look of the dish long before she began to cook. This process is called *"prepping."*

Although she was deep in thought, she was never bogged down with too many details. Instead, she continually applied her creative intelligence to work with the ingredients she had on hand, and before long, a mouthwatering aroma filled the air from the kitchen, and then a wonderful dish emerged, cooked to perfection.

In our daily lives, the complexity and challenges we encounter are similar to the various spices used in creating the above dish because they add flavor and character to our life experiences. My 9 Moms always reminded me that life's happiness is not a destination but rather the journey itself. Therefore, I always *"live to learn, to love, and to leave a legacy."*

Ask any great chef, and he or she will tell you that all great recipes survive through the generations and will continue to be handed down to future generations in each family. Although some of these recipes have been modified and refined over the years, they still have their core integrity as far as flavor, taste, and appeal.

Just as my mom, Eleanora, would say, *"A good cooking recipe mirrors life. It is never static. It always needs to be able to change to keep pace with the flavor and taste buds of the day."*

It is my sincere desire and hope that when you read the various *"recipes for living,"* they will rekindle some endearing, wonderful memories of you and your mom and perhaps other loved ones who had been instrumental in helping you navigate your life's journey to experience success in all areas of your life. By the way, the good news is that these recipes are evergreen, timeless wisdom about life, love, and laughter! So, don't hesitate to share them with your personal touch and experiences to help the next generation in their life's journey to experiencing happiness, blessings, and abundance.

1. Time Is A Luxury We All Have

I will always remember what my mom, Carol, told me when we first met. She said, *"Time is a luxury we all have."* It is often said that no time is the right time, and any time is the right time. To have faith that the right thing will come along at the right time and in the right way is an indulgence that we absolutely should make room for in our lives.

Johnny Tan

As we hold on to this belief, it will make passing up situations that are not a good fit for us a lot easier. Over the years, I have had numerous experiences in my professional and personal life where this simple yet profound advice saved me from potential agony had I not taken the time. I am surprised not because of the resulting circumstances but rather how insightful Carol's advice is. What seems to be an excellent idea and opportunity at first, especially with all the "bells and whistles," gradually fades away as it did not endure the test of time.

Carol, Me, and Nyah

2. The Dance Of Life—Are We Following, Or Are We Leading?

My mom, Betty, told me years ago that dancing is always from the heart, as it requires passion and commitment. Echoing my mom Nyah's sentiments, like in life and in dancing, I cannot achieve a full-time reward with a part-time effort.

One of the most insightful lessons I learned from Betty is that although the perception about the world of dancing is that the men always lead and the women always follow; however, this is not true. The men initiate the pattern, and the women dance their part to complete it. The lead, however, comes from whoever steps forward because the forward momentum is the most crucial energy in executing a beautiful pattern perfectly.

For example, in dancing the Waltz Box pattern, the man leads off by taking a 3-foot forward step with his left foot and then with his right foot steps 3 feet to his right, which is referred to as the "top of the box." Now, it is the lady's turn to complete the second half of the box. To do so, she is to step forward with her left foot as the man initiates it with a backward step with his right foot. However, if she only stepped 2 feet forward, we ended up with a Waltz Rectangle pattern instead of the Waltz Box pattern.

Funny as it may be, the moral of the story is to clearly show that *"situation"* dictates who takes the lead! The man (who is the leader) initiates the pattern; he leads when he steps forward and to his right. But when he steps backward, his role is now the "follower." It is the lady's turn to take the lead and finish the pattern beautifully as intended.

In the dance of life, regardless of our position, a corporate executive or manager or frontline staff, a husband or a wife, the *"situation"* at hand will always dictate who takes the lead, especially when it comes to team synergy. The most successful formula I used as the COO of a multi-level management structure with 600+ employees, which I later used in my keynote and workshop presentations, is *"We Lead People, We Manage Situation."* No one likes to be managed.

However, everyone is open to being led. So, let the *"situation"* at hand dictate who leads and who follows. By the way, when you follow, be the best follower you can be because the trick is that in order to be a good leader, you first need to be a good follower. You now have your heart, mind, body, and spirit in alignment with life's rhythm.

3. Something Interesting About Fortune Cookies

I remember my mom, Elsa Mae, telling me years ago that when reading a fortune cookie, you should always read to learn and not read to rebuff. She went on to explain that our mood or present circumstance has a lot to do with our final take on the fortune we receive. It is true that the cookies are factory-made, and the fortune messages are generated by a computer and put into the cookies by machines; however, we receive our cookies by random selection, which means there is a touch of the unknown involved that could be a little mystifying.

Ordinary folks like us, just wonder if sometimes the fortune we receive is truly meant to be a reflection of the past, a snapshot of the present, or perhaps a preview of the future.

Regardless of which one it is, one thing for sure is that it is meant to be a pick-me-up, perhaps thought-provoking, and if nothing else, a fun after-meal conversation topic.

I can only speak for myself when I say this—regardless of how I am feeling at any given moment, I can always use a little good news to brighten and enhance my day. I once received a fortune cookie that read, "*Genius does what it must, and Talent does what it can.*"

This phrase reminded me of what my mom Nyah, told me when I first started working. She said, *"In every one of us there is a seed of greatness. This seed of greatness holds the key to all our successes. The Genius in us helps us to identify our goals, dreams, and desires, and the Talent in us helps us to accomplish them with a heartfelt passion."*

However, just because we have this seed of greatness does not guarantee us greatness and success. It is what we do with it that will ultimately determine our success. This means that we can all live a perfect life if we choose to, and if we apply ourselves by using the knowledge that we learn from within and from the lessons we learn along our life journeys, we can certainly achieve our desired success.

4. The Essence Of Making A Change

Change may sometimes start out as being difficult because the first step is always the scariest one, but eventually, it is for the best if we continue to focus on the final desired outcome.

When we are fixated on a target, everything else falls away as each step takes us closer to our goal, and the path to the final destination will unveil itself.

Whenever I was in a difficult situation, my mom, Toni, always reminded me of this: *"What the caterpillar refers to as the end of the world, the butterfly calls it the beginning of a beautiful life."*

This recipe for living has helped me better understand that life only goes in one direction: *"Forward."* Yesterday's experience will always contribute to Today's planning for a Better Tomorrow!

5. Having A Balanced Approach To Everything

We may not realize this, but we are actually living in a closed system—that is, we cannot create order without creating disorder elsewhere. Living too much to the right or to the left of life's spectrum will eventually result in an unbalanced and unhealthy lifestyle.

My mom, Elsa Mae, told me that in order to maintain a balanced approach to everything in life, I must use my brain and my heart synergistically. This allows us to be simultaneously elegant and goofy, silly and serious, and loving and critical. The trick is to allow ourselves to move naturally and freely throughout the entire spectrum of possibilities. We have now created *"a quiet bubble of confidence"* around us, which allows us to formulate our actions after effectively evaluating the current situation.

6. Being Present In The Present Moment

Sometimes, in our busy lives, we tend to forget to focus on the *present moment*. Our minds tend to drift ahead of us, thinking far off into the future with the *what-ifs*. At other times, we are caught up in reminiscing about events of the past. If it is a good reflection, then we always wish we could replay it over again and again, but if it is a bad memory, we tend to be weighed down with disappointments.

If we are not careful, we may miss the opportunity of enjoying today. To ensure that this does not happen, we need to be present in the *present moment*. We cannot change what happened yesterday, and we can only dream about tomorrow. However, we can certainly affect today by being conscious of our present thoughts.

I am always reminded of what my mom, Dee, told me: *"Yesterday is gone, and tomorrow may never come. One thing for sure is that we have today, and what we do with it will determine how we will be remembered tomorrow."*

My friend Kat gave me this prayer years ago, and since then, I have used it daily to remind myself to always be *"present in today."* I would like to share it with you, and I hope that it will bring to you the daily peaceful, quiet confidence it brought me.

A Spiritual Growth Affirmation
(Author unknown)

*My inner wisdom grows stronger and clearer,
every day in every way.*

*I am a clear channel of love and light;
I am well-guided both day and night.*

*I hereby release any previous distrust
of my own judgment and decisions.*

*I now trust my higher self to guide me well.
I open [my] mind and heart and
now perceive all higher guidance that I receive.*

*I release former fears and send them away.
I am calm; I am still; my heart and life, God-Light does fill.
Everything I am and do is through God.*

7. Overcoming Fear

Sometimes, things may not work out as planned because the timing is off. If we have given our best, then we have to release it to the universe to be sorted out.

According to my mom Nyah, *"Life and situations have a way of working themselves out eventually through a universal order. If we believe in faith and live our lives with full expectancy, then we can trust that all things will work out for our greatest good."*

Over the years, I have learned this to be true because whenever I did just that, I was rewarded greatly for not fearing letting go and not being in control.

A friend once told me that she has the ability to talk herself out of just about anything due to her tremendous amount of control over her mind. This is good; however, if not used or exercised correctly, it can bring about the opposite effect of what this gift is intended for.

If we use it to run away from our fears, then we are not utilizing it for the right reason; we are actually giving into our weaknesses. My mom, Nyah, said it best: *"As easily as we can talk ourselves out of something, we can talk ourselves into something."*

It is the essence of the *power of positive thinking*, talking ourselves into confronting and overcoming our fears, that strengthens our overall being, which in turn moves us to the next level of personal excellence.

My mom, Eleanora, believed that perseverance and patience would always help us overcome personal self-inflicted anxiety. According to her, you should never be afraid to change your mind. Admitting mistakes rather than standing firm on an ill-informed decision actually shows maturity, intelligence, and character.

Whenever I had doubts about certain issues I was dealing with that required a leap of faith, I always reminded myself of what my mom, Betty, said to me over the years, quoting from her favorite movie line from the movie Strictly Ballroom, *"A life lived in fear is a life half lived."*

She said that when we learn to empower ourselves to change the way we look at things, we are actually learning to know our inner selves. When we realize that the power in us is greater than the one outside, then we are ready to change our situation. When positive changes come from the inside out, we have attained the right positive vision.

> ***In a Nutshell****—The key to overcoming fear is to have the right positive vision that has been within us all along.*

8. The Art Of Being A Good Listener

A friend once asked me to explain the difference between hearing and listening. I told her the difference is that when we listen to someone, we are engaging ourselves to truly learn what he or she is trying to relate to us, rather than just hearing words coming out of someone's mouth and hearing what we want to hear instead.

In today's world of multitasking, we are all guilty of doing too many things at the same time just because we can, or perhaps just because we are multitalented. In order to truly build a good and everlasting habit of being a good listener, which adds value to any communication, we will need to practice something my mom, Elsa

Mae, used to tell me a long time ago. *"When we listen to someone, listen to learn, and do not listen in anticipation to reply."*

In other words, when we listen to learn, we are listening and learning about what we can do to meet their needs, whereas when we are just hearing, we are simply waiting for the opportunity to pawn off our opinion to them. We are caught up in the *"if I were you, I would do..."* syndrome.

Guess what? We will always be who we are, and they will always be who they are. Each of us is different from the perspective of our own individualism—our very own upper and lower limits. Each of us is governed by our own strengths and weaknesses and by our comfort zone.

We all operate at our best when we are in our comfort zone, so it is important to study that person's needs before we can truly give our best input. In order to do this, we must make sure we give them our undivided attention. We need to be respectful and considerate of the person's style of conveying his or her message to us.

Our actions and demeanor speak volumes about this. Someone can easily tell if we are just trying to pacify them or if we are genuinely trying to help by effectively listening to them. A good rule of thumb to follow is—are we being selfish, or are we adding value to our communication? If we intend to add value, then we will give our input with love and tactfulness because we are saying things to benefit them and not us.

Another excellent approach to effective communication is *"Listening to someone into existence."* I have used this approach very successfully since I was a teenager. What the hack is this? Well, remember when you felt furious, whether when you were a child or now as an adult, trying to get someone to listen to you and have your story heard, but no one seems to care about hearing what you have to say! Yup! This is it! Wouldn't it have been great if the person you were trying to talk to gave you the undivided attention and time you need to express what you have to say and get it out of your system, so to speak? This is what *"listening to someone into existence"* means. The beauty of this approach is that you gain their respect and trust, even though you may not agree with everything they have to say. The magical reason is that you made them feel special and that they *"Matter"* because you took the time to genuinely listen to what they had to say!

> ***In a Nutshell**—The art of being a good listener is nothing more than being genuine, sincere, and giving undivided attention to the person who is talking to us.*

9. Annual rebirths

When I was 15 years old, my mom, Nyah, taught me about my personal new year, my once-a-year opportunity to regroup and relaunch myself. It is my *"annual rebirth"* for my heart, mind, body, and spirit. I learned that I can't change the past. However, I can create the future I want with better planning by utilizing today, this moment in time, to map out what I want going forward.

She also told me that the day we stop learning is the day we give up on living. Since then, every year, days before my birthday, I have used quiet moments to reflect upon all the hits and misses in my life during the past 12 months. From a simple review to contemplating life-changing experiences, the introspection provided me with *"A Rear View Vision of the Opportunities and Possibilities Ahead."* There are no mistakes, instead lessons. Nor are there failures, only setbacks. If I don't know what went wrong and take ownership, I can't effectively proceed forward successfully! I eventually learned to identify potential opportunities on not only how to live my life but also how to live my life with passion in the upcoming year by adjusting my thought process and my behavioral tendencies. The rebirthing process helped to fill me with a renewed spirit, ideas, and enthusiasm.

Over the years, interestingly enough, halfway around the world in the US, my various moms also had some excellent nuggets of advice for me when I asked them for their insights about navigating my upcoming year.

My mom, Carol, taught me, *"Once we acknowledge that our true nature is more than a few personality traits, interests, and experiences, we will understand that what makes us essentially unique is that we are capable of changing our tomorrow by using yesterday as a point of reference and today as the launching pad for hope."* She also added, *"Wisdom is what we experience when we combine knowledge, understanding, and compassion."*

My mom, Dee, taught me, *"Luck is the intersection of faith and destiny. The stronger our faith is, the luckier we are. The positive energy we radiate into the universe will always attract like positive energy back to us."*

My mom, Elsa Mae, taught me, *"Words Have Power! So, what we express is what we will receive in return. Since we are the author of our thoughts, if we want to receive and be showered with good things and favors in life, we need to be those positive thoughts throughout our daily lives."*

I have been fortunate to have successfully reached the top of my personal Mount Everest in my early thirties. However, due to unforeseen circumstances, I also experienced the sudden plunge to the bottom of the Grand Canyon of Life in my late forties. The most profound advice I hold dear and close to my heart every year during my annual rebirthing process is what my mom, Nyah, always reminded me whenever I am feeling flat after having the wind sucked out of my sail. She said, *"We create our own little world where we want to live. However, outside circumstances will always affect our daily lives."* She continued, *"To stay focused, we need to remind ourselves—We are not the product of our environment, but rather, our environment is the product of who we are!"*

Whether it is pure chance or divine guidance, I have experienced significant increases in luck and wisdom in all areas of my life by keeping my mind focused on having hope, believing in faith, and viewing life through the lens of love in my daily meditation.

10. The Answers Are All Around Us

My mom, Elsa Mae, once told me that *"true love and true friendship last a lifetime."* If we truly pay attention to the people we meet and the people who come into our lives, we will find they are there for a reason. Some people are in our lives for just a short stay, some for a season, and some for a lifetime.

When people come into our lives for just a short stay, it is usually to meet our current immediate needs. They have come to be with us to provide support, fellowship, and guidance to assist us in overcoming our current life challenges and crises.

Having our prayers answered, we see their arrival as a Godsend; however, their stay is short. When our needs and desires have been met and fulfilled, and their presence is no longer needed, their departure is as sudden as their appearance in our lives. As thankful as we are for this brief encounter, we, too, should be ready to move on.

For those who come for a season, the time we spend with them engages and exposes us to something new and different. Although their presence brings about some fun and thrilling times as they bring experiences of joy, peace, and laughter into our lives, these sharing, growth, and learning moments are only for a season.

Then, there are people who come into our lives to teach us lifelong lessons. When we embrace these special relationships and the infinite wisdom they offer, we can better ourselves in all areas of our lives. The lessons learned will enable us to build solid foundations for our *physical, emotional, and spiritual well-being*, which lasts a lifetime.

11. The Power Of Positive Visualization

Whenever I am working on a new project, whether in my professional or personal life, I have to remind myself what my mom, Betty, told me when she first taught me ballroom dancing. Her advice was that *"successful people always visualize their successes long before they actually attain them."*

By creating a perfect picture in our subconscious mind of what we want whenever we come face-to-face with a challenge, we are actually programming our successes from the inside out.

Although our desire to be happy and successful originates from the heart, we still have to create an image of what we want to achieve in our subconscious mind in order to bring it to fruition.

Our subconscious mind, which, by the way, never sleeps, does not know the difference between what is real and what is not. It just registers all the images we visualize and serves as a blueprint for us. The images from our subconscious mind are always flawless and perfect.

It is our constant visualization of these right images in our subconscious mind that activates the right attitude and passion within ourselves to produce the desired result. Studies have shown that many "*faith-based healing*" have resulted from this technique where science does not have an explanation for such successful results.

From a personal and business management perspective, our personal and corporate vision statements are powerful tools we can use to set the right mindset for achieving what we seek or desire to achieve.

When we realize that we are the architect and programmer of our path to success, we can start filling our subconscious minds with the right positive image of success in all areas of our lives. As we consistently play and replay this right positive image daily, before long, a manifestation of a new positive habit will start to take root within our mind, body, and spirit, energized by our heart.

12. The Various Seasons Of Our Life

The Harvest Full Moon is the full moon nearest to the autumnal equinox, which symbolically marks the beginning of the autumn season. It also reminds me of what my mom, Nyah, who grew up in the rice fields of Melaka, Malaysia, used to tell me about the various seasons that we go through in life.

From a farming perspective—*we have the plowing season, the planting season, the watering season, and the harvesting season.* How well the land is plowed will determine the type of crop that can be planted on it, and how well the crop is watered will determine the size and bountifulness of the harvest.

Likewise, our daily routine goes through various seasons each year as we move through life. How well we prepare our *"inner self"* will determine the type of project we will accomplish, and how well we nurture it will determine the level of success we will achieve.

Throughout the plowing, planting, and watering seasons, we will always be challenged and given choices we need to make. These decisions will undoubtedly affect the outcome of the harvest.

"Timing is everything." If we make the right move at the right time, we will be ensured the predictable successes that follow because of our foresight to see beyond today. Seizing this given moment can make every setback into the turning point of a comeback.

If we pay attention to the little voices within us and rise to move at the right time, and when each task becomes a labor of love performed with much creativity, then we are seizing the opportunity to propel ourselves to the next level of excellence.

13. The Synergy Of The Heart And The Mind

My mom, Nyah, taught me how to use my heart in everything I do. She said that thinking about something is just a simple thought, and it cannot become more than a thought unless it is acted on.

However, to have a vision of success is to have dreams and desires that always come from the heart. Therefore, it always has passion, and when passion is initiated, the mind will follow the heart and will always find a way to fulfill the passion.

> ***In a Nutshell**—Thinking is preparing to succeed. Going from thinking to feeling is acting upon an unwavering, passionate commitment to make it into a reality.*

14. Living A Mindful Life

My mom, Toni, once told me that each one of us has an outer life and an inner life. The outer life is our public life that everyone can see. It is made up of social interactions, whereas our inner life is made up of our thoughts, our attitudes, and our motives.

Only we know what is going on inside our inner life. Many times, we go around pretending or acting one way, yet on the inside, we are thinking something totally different. Our hearts and our actions just do not quite line up.

Whether these actions mask our own insecurities or—worse—hide our sinister motives, we can only fool people some of the time, but not all the time. Since true friendships and relationships are built on openness and honesty, we need to realize and understand that we are looked at from the inside out.

Although it is true that we live essentially a subjective life—*where one's graffiti is another's artwork, and one's riveting avant-garde music is another's noise*—ultimately, we know from within ourselves the true petition of our hearts in all matters at hand.

If we are mindful and find peace and comfort in all of our actions and behavior in whatever we say or do, then we have performed selflessly for ourselves and, most importantly, for the greater good of others, and this is Karma at its best.

15. Character-Driven Living

My mom, Nyah, always said that it is during the challenging times of our lives that our authentic character is built, and we are getting stronger from the inside out. Everything has a season. Everything has its time.

My mom, Eleanora, has always reminded me that life is not always as smooth as we would like it to be. It is how we step up to face the sudden, unanticipated challenges we are confronted with that truly build and forge our overall authentic personal character.

If we are aware and mindful enough to allow this to happen, our faith can then lead us to the knowledge that everything is meant to make us better as we construct and build our character to help us navigate all areas of our lives.

She went on to say, "*Our authentic charm and personality may open doors for us; however, it is our authentic integrity character that keeps them open.*"

16. Having A Sense Of Humor In Everything We Do

Have you ever considered that someone's brilliant oneliner may tickle you more than your funny bone because it may ignite a tiny spark in your heart? If this is true about you, then you are one of the few people who can truly appreciate and realize that having fun and being funny can lead you to live a very healthy and romantic life.

My mom, Ginger, believes that humor is essential in our daily lives because it brings balance and a sense of humility to us when we face challenging situations or demanding people. She says, *"With humor, we can always look and find the lighter side of things to be positive, regardless of whatever we encounter."*

The choices we make, whether to be serious or to have a touch of humor in anything we do, speak loudly to others about our personality and who we are. How we are perceived by others is how they would rate us verbally or nonverbally regarding our credibility, trustworthiness, and sense of responsibility.

Although the accuracy of this kind of assessment done by others on us can be questionable, however, if we think about it, we do the same thing. Perhaps not as elaborate or thorough as others might see us, but at the very least, we do have an impression of others as to how they view life.

If we come across as funny and lighthearted and can somehow find humor in anything, then we are likely to be perceived as *kind, gentle, confident, and lovable.*

In actuality, all of these do wonders for our very own physical well-being, as we are likely to be less stressed because we just enjoy living life without taking it too seriously. If laughter is not simply the best medicine, it is certainly one of life's saving graces.

17. The Art Of Moving Forward With Our Lives

One of the toughest things in life is to leave past mistakes and missteps behind as water under the bridge. We should not allow them to distract us while we are thinking about designing our future successes.

If we are to move forward in our professional or personal lives, we have to believe that events of the past were stepping stones and lessons that prepared and helped us to become who we are currently, positioning us to be at the right place and at the right time to embark on a new course in our life's journey.

My mom, Betty, is considered an angelic person by those who have known her personally. She was always there for everyone. She was enthusiastic about life and believed that the glass was never half empty or half full; rather, it always had room to be topped off with something fresh and new.

With this approach of open-mindedness coupled with the strong attitude that *anything is possible*, we are empowering ourselves to take chances that we might not have otherwise been willing to take. By combining positive thinking and living life with full expectancy, we are now equipped to attempt new things and situations in life.

By avoiding the mantra that everything has to be mastered or conquered, we give ourselves an opportunity to enjoy the process of "*being in the process*" rather than self-inflicting ourselves with the pressure that everything has to be just right and perfect.

Accepting that the world and everyone living in it, including ourselves, are not perfect, we can now shift our energy and attention toward enjoying our daily journey rather than arriving at some elusive utopian destination.

As my mom, Betty, would remind me, *"When we acknowledge to ourselves and take ownership that we are the author of our life, then perfection and happiness will be what we want them to be, rather than what we think others perceive them to be."*

18. Creating The Right First Impression

My mom, Nyah, always said that being a mom is all about making a positive difference in her children's lives. Whether by nature or by instinct, I believe all moms have the same tendency to do just that.

Taking this a step further, whenever we encounter someone, we will always affect his or her life in some way. This impact can be *"verbal or nonverbal."* If we are mindful of this, then we can plan to make each impact a positive one.

More often than not, it is the *nonverbal impact* that gives others their first impression of us. The *verbal impact* that follows is more of a validation of their first impression, or it will nullify it completely, which sometimes can be bad for us.

19. The Art Of Planning Future Successes

In planning future successes, there is no right or wrong; rather, choices are made to best address the current situation at hand. Whether there was a lesson to be learned or just another episode of running away from our very own insecurities, only history and hindsight will reveal that to us in due season.

Johnny Tan

My mom, Dee, used to tell me all the time, *"In planning for future successes in all areas of our lives, always use history and old memories as a reference of where we were, where we had been, and what we had experienced."*

It should always be a point of *reference* but never a guide. If it is used as a guide, then the future never changes. However, if it is used as a point of *reference*, then the future will always be fresh and new as we make it to be.

According to my mom, Carol, occasionally, we cannot help but reminisce about old memories from past events in our lives. Although memories are lovely and should be appreciated, we need to be careful not to start living in the past. While our relationships and various events were built and took place under certain conditions and under certain expectations, *everything is everchanging*, including people.

In planning future successes, my mom Nyah taught me that all changes do not have to be abrupt, shocking, or awe-inspiring; rather, *it is more about making small shifts that will result in permanent, rooted changes within us.*

If we look deep within ourselves, we will find that we, too, are not exempt from experiencing changes from within. Whether we are moving forward, sideways, or in reverse, we are not immune to changing our opinions, our beliefs, and our take on life. This is because we all have *"Free Will"* to follow what we think is best for ourselves.

Unfortunately, what may be the best for us may not be the best for others, and likewise, what may be the best for others may not necessarily be the best for us. Sometimes, a person may be labeled selfish when his or her decision benefits them; however, we are not privy to the thought process they used to arrive at that decision. No one absolutely knows what is truly in the heart of hearts of that individual. Whether someone fits the label of being selfish or unselfish is ultimately up to the individual person who has to make that tough decision.

20. The Dance Of Life—The Synergy Of Oneness

Is life always as clear as black and white, or is it various shades of gray? This was a topic of discussion I had with my German mom, Dianne, a few years ago.

She is my youngest mom, at 86 years young! We have known each other for several months since I met her and her husband, Bill, through the various ballroom dancing events we were in attendance. However, our relationship did not begin until we were invited to perform with our husband-and-wife dance instructors, Danny and Sandy Schmidt. It was a Waltz seminar weekend in Biloxi, Mississippi, in 1998, where she performed a quickstep routine with Danny, and I was there to perform a Bolero routine with Sandy.

Having some quality time to visit, we soon discovered that besides doing ballroom dancing and having mutual friends, we both enjoyed cooking very much. She and her husband (they recently celebrated their forty-seventh wedding anniversary) are also avid gardeners. They pretty much grow their own vegetables for personal consumption. This is a carryover from their longing for fresh organic fruits and vegetables, which they grew accustomed to while they were living in Brussels, Belgium, and in Port Jerome, a town in Normandy, France, in the late 1960s. This was when

Bill, who was working as a chemical engineer for Esso (present-day ExxonMobil), was transferred to their European division for a six-month assignment.

Although Dianne and I realized and appreciated the existence of both variations in any human relationship is good, we agreed that there should be a system for both variations to give relationships an added catalyst to weather the daily challenges of living together.

A little touch of organization is always necessary to give any relationship the magical versatility it needs to achieve long-term, sustainable success. Although initially, we may fear that the *"magic of the relationship"* will disappear or be lost in a set-up system, in all actuality, it does not.

Sure, things may feel different for a little while in the beginning, but we should remain mindful that sometimes one of us needs to be the rudder, and the other needs to be the engine in the relationship. Therefore, by continually focusing on the big picture of the highest good for the *"both of us,"* then, the entire journey will always be blessed with a wave of selflessness and trusting thoughts.

In the dance of life, this altruistic attitude from both partners will give birth to a deeper level of love, understanding, and appreciation of each other that can be best described as a perfect synergy of both souls, where both will experience the bliss and harmony of *"Oneness."*

As love and happiness in any relationship are experienced by *"the moment,"* in the dance of life, true love and true happiness are *"blissful moments"* that last a lifetime.

21. Defining Ourselves

Recently, a friend said she knows what she wants in her life; however, she has difficulty defining herself. Years earlier, my mom, Betty, advised me that in order to define myself, I have to look within and take a *"personal inventory."*

This personal inventory is an honest assessment of myself through my very own eyes—my innermost feelings about everything. Only I know my true self—my weaknesses, strengths, likes, dislikes, confidence, insecurities, what turns me on, what turns me off, my values, and my spiritual beliefs.

What we want, which are our goals and our ambitions, are our mission. Who we are and what we do are actually our personal visions and values for our lives, which in turn help to define us. We will have many missions in life because as we accomplish one mission, we will move on to the next one. However, our personal vision/our personal character will never change. It will always go through refinements, but it will never change.

Knowing our personal vision and values is important because they are *the essence of our existence*. According to my mom, Toni, until we truly know who we are, we cannot effectively know what we truly want in life. I am sure you have been asked these questions before, "What do you see yourself doing about this situation?" or "What do you see yourself doing X years from now?" The *"see"* in both questions refers to your *"personal vision and values."*

> ***In a Nutshell**—What we see is what we get—our character, our convictions, our values, and our beliefs. It is all of these combined*

with our behavior tendencies, which is what we do, that define us. Once we know who we are and our personal vision, we can then truly invoke the powers of The Law of Attraction to work for us every time to achieve whatever we seek in life.

22. The Power Of Having The Right Friends And Associates

I have always been taught that *"I am the reflection of the company of friends and people with whom I keep and associate with."* Whether this reflection is good or bad, it will give others the opportunity to decide whether to associate with me and keep me in their inner circle as a close friend.

According to my mom, Carol, although we may not have much of a choice when it comes to family members and relatives, however, we always have a choice when it comes to friends. This freedom of choice gives us the opportunity to surround ourselves with individuals who can help us stay motivated and achieve whatever it is we aspire to achieve in both our professional and personal lives.

By associating ourselves with individuals who draw the best out of us and who have the ability to teach and motivate us, whether directly or indirectly, we are building a strong foundation for our future successes.

As we embrace education as a part of our daily life journey, we can then open our minds and accept the fact that we *"do not know it all."* We are now ready to learn something new every day. Interestingly enough, when we realize this about ourselves, we will start to take notice that we, too, are being sought after by other individuals who, like us, want to surround themselves with like-minded individuals who can help them achieve their full potential through their association with us.

> ***In a Nutshell**—After defining what we want to accomplish in life, we can now author our lives with a passionate desire to include the circle of friends and associates who we believe can help us in our journey to achieving our personal excellence and success.*

23. Inner Power—The Magic From Within

A few years ago, my mom, Carol, emailed me an article that helped me understand that I have the magic within me to transform myself from the inside out spiritually. Her email was in response to my renewed interest in exploring the benefits of meditation and how I was going to incorporate it into my daily routine.

I would like to share this article, *Inner Power*, with you and hope that you will get as much out of it as I did when I first read it.

Inner Power
(Author Unknown)

*Inner power is divine love, and
it is a natural expression of our humanness.*

When we open our mouth to speak, we anticipate that words will come out and that these words will convey the meaning we intend.

When we open our heart to feel love for others, we will experience unlimited and unconditional love.

The deeply personal and profound feelings that come through meditation, as well as through intimate and direct experiences of loving our partner, our children, and our friends, are the natural state of our humanness and are the basis of our spiritual leadership.

Inner power is resilient. It is expressed as empathy for other living things, and it comes forth as nonjudgmental grace.

Resilience teaches us to observe our life from a different and deeper perspective, thus enabling us to move around the constraints of pain and loss.

Empathy teaches us to trust our natural desire to help others and, in return, to receive love from people, nature, and God.

Living in grace allows us to teach others through the example of our own life, and to offer nourishment through awareness of divine love in action in our life, and on the Earth.

24. A Purpose-Driven Life

It was certainly a tremendous treat for me to have had the opportunity to meet with Danica McKellar, the actress, mathematics writer, and education advocate, twice in less than 24 months. This time around is because she was in Dallas, promoting her book *Math Doesn't Suck*. It has been about a year since we last met on one of her *Inspector Mom* movie sets, which was filmed in Dallas, Texas.

Always full of energy and enthusiasm, Danica is an excellent role model for impressionable young minds when it comes to making a difference in their lives. It is during moments like this that I am reminded of what my mom, Dee, told me a long time ago when I asked her this question, *"What is my destiny?"*

She said that it was something for me to find out for myself. However, she added, *"One thing for sure is that we were all put here on earth to make a lasting impression on others. Whether we choose to make a positive or negative impression is up to us. Nonetheless, we will leave a personal impression on others."*

Since 1996, I have made a personal commitment through my vision and mission statements to be a positive role model for others with whom I am fortunate to have the opportunity to cross paths. It has not been easy at times because we are all human, and we all have our moments of ups and downs.

However, if we continually remind ourselves that we are here to make a difference in someone else's life, a positive difference at that, then it is not difficult for us to always deliver on this pledge if we put the needs of others ahead of our own.

If we are mindful and respectful of others, then we will always be an asset and a catalyst for them in their pursuit of their purpose-driven life.

25. Sometimes, A Chance Encounter Can Bring Great Meaning To Our Lives

I first met my good friend Maureen at the United States Amateur Ballroom Dancers Association event in Dallas in November 2003. I was scouting the city with the intention of moving my business there. She and her dance partner, Byron, were sitting next to me.

I was taken with her and Byron's dancing skills and later asked her for a dance. As I took her around the dance floor, we started to talk about our dancing skills and techniques and where and from whom they were taking lessons.

I told her about my lessons with my mom, Betty, and she told me that she and Byron were currently taking lessons from a world-class International Latin Ballroom Dance Champion couple, Shorena Gachechiladze and Gocha Chertkoev. Impressed but not intimidated by her answer, I proceeded to respond nonverbally—I let my lead and dancing skills do the talking.

By the end of the evening, she was impressed with my skills and invited me to check out her dance studio. I took her up on the offer upon relocating myself and my business to Dallas in January 2004. After a formal meeting with Shorena and Gocha, I decided to become their student.

Danica and Me

Through them, I met Danica McKellar in the fall of 2006 when she came to Dallas to film her *Inspector Mom* TV movie series. I was fortunate enough to have been selected to be one of the ballroom dancers in one of her episodes, *"Kidnapped in Ten Easy Steps."*

I have always been intrigued by the world of blogging, especially while in the process of writing the first edition of my From My Mama's Kitchen - "food for the soul, recipes for living" book. In the late summer of 2007, upon doing some research, I came across a couple of successful bloggers, John Chow and Penelope Trunk. After reading their respective sites, I was encouraged to give it a try, and I started blogging for a few months. The experience I gained from blogging was tremendously helpful as it literally kept me focused on my writing, which led me to finish writing my book by the end of that year.

I remember my mom, Eleanora, telling me this, *"To the world, you may be just one person, but to one person, you may be the world. It is always the small shifts one goes through in life that result in an everlasting, positive, rooted transformation."*

26. Hearing The Rest Of The Story

In early 2005, through a friend's connection, he and I had an impromptu meeting with a business manager of an establishment with whom we were looking into a collaborative business partnership. As one would expect, we discussed many things during the meeting. However, what stood out the most after the meeting was not what the business manager had said and shared but rather what the business manager had not said to us.

As a former successful young COO, during our sidebar discussion to summarize the meeting, I pointed out a few subtle but important points for us to consider. We realized that all we had heard was ambiguity and lack of personal substance. What we actually needed to hear was what we did not hear, which helped us to make an informed decision.

Sometimes, in life, we can learn much more from what is not said rather than from what is said. I remember what my mom, Carol, told me a long time ago about always paying attention to what people do not say in order to get *"the rest of the story."*

Her advice is that, often, in conversations concerning sensitive issues, it is not uncommon for people to tell us what they want us to hear rather than what we need to hear. If we pay attention to what is *"not said,"* we can then get the rest of the story.

I could not quite understand it at that time, but over the years, after having encountered situations similar to the one above, I now know exactly what she meant. Having honed my *"listening skills,"* I am now always tuned in to getting the rest of the story, which has enabled me to make better, well-informed decisions.

> **Food for Thought:** *If we believe we can all learn from hearing what is not said along with what is said to get the rest of the story when we truly pay attention to whom we are talking with, are they also as mindful as we are, that is, hearing what is not said by us, too?*

27. A Recipe For Writing

A fascinating concept I have learned about writing comes from a book by Joel Saltzman titled *If You Can Talk, You Can Write*. It taught me to talk on paper without worrying about whether it is good or bad; rather, it is about just letting my energetic, creative, true self go and feeling free to express myself in an entertaining way.

I also learned from another source the following writing recipe for being a successful writer. It states that in order for a book to be successful, it has to have the following ingredients. It needs to have emotion, passion, bonding, and fun.

> **Emotion**—It needs to have feelings.
>
> **Passion**—It needs to come from the heart.
>
> **Bonding**—It needs to engage the readers.
>
> **Fun**—It needs to be entertaining.

I find that the above writing recipe is truly applicable to everyday living, too, as it reminded me of what my mom, Ginger, used to tell me about living our daily lives. She said, *"We need emotion to feel about others and ourselves. We need passion to sustain a drive while pursuing our goals and dreams. We need bonding to be inclusive rather than exclusive in making effective decisions. We need fun and humor to entertain ourselves in order to keep us balanced and grounded."*

28. Education Will Always Be Part Of Our Life's Journey

If we believe in success, then we must believe that education should always be a part of our life's journey. When we open our minds and accept the fact that we do not know it all, and we never will, we are positioning ourselves to be ready to learn something new and add a new facet to our knowledge bank.

By embracing this concept and logic, things will go much smoother for us. We now have a greater understanding that sometimes it is not who we know but rather what we know that gives us the competitive edge in all areas of our lives. When we are equipped with the right information, we will actually attract many more people into our circle of contacts.

According to my mom, Dianne, *"Amazingly enough, until we try to teach someone else, we usually do not even realize that we have all the knowledge that is readily available from within us. As we impart a lesson to others, we will also be learning something new about ourselves in the process, as well."*

29. The Art Of Turning A Job Into A Career

When does our job become a career? This was one of the topics my seatmate, Leigh, and I talked about while flying from Salt Lake City, Utah, to San Francisco, California, a few years ago.

I started out by saying that a job is something we do to pay our bills, whereas a career is a hobby we do and we get paid for, and more often than not, we get paid very well, too. We both agreed that in order to experience this *"career/hobby"* feeling, we need to be passionate about what we do.

Leigh, in the past 30 years, did just that. While we were talking, I clearly saw the enthusiasm and passion she has for her current career. Can we have more than one career in our lifetime? The answer is yes, absolutely!

It is not what we do that defines our career; it is how and the way we do it that defines our career. Whenever we approach and apply passionate enthusiasm to whatever we are doing, we elevate it to a career status.

It is our attitude that drives us into our careers. We must have a positive and engaging attitude that puts people first because, regardless of whatever profession we are in, we are always in the *"People Business."* Once we realize this, our positive energy will be contagious, and it will affect everyone around us in a positive manner.

However, if we are disengaged and don't really care about making a difference in someone's life, or just have the attitude of "Hey, I am here, aren't I?" or are only monetarily driven, then the entire "about us" body language and demeanor, will tell everyone that we are just putting in our time or we are just in it for the money.

My mom, Dee, in the many conversations we had about work, reminded me a long time ago that *"regardless of what we are currently doing, we should always give it our best because we never know who is watching us."*

She is absolutely right; I personally have experienced this, as I happened to pay attention to how my team members/employees carry themselves while doing their daily assignments. Hold and behold, you will be surprised that some gave their all, whereas others are only putting in their time, so to speak. Those who expressed their genuine thoroughness daily in their approach to getting their work done were self-motivated. To complement their enthusiasm, I created special training classes to further help them excel in their personal lives and, more importantly, enhance their chances for upward mobility when opportunities arise within our company as we grow and expand.

Food for Thought: By being conscious of the present moment and committed to doing things right and doing the right thing every time, we will always be ready to receive whatever positive breaks might come our way when we least expect them.

30. Taking The Right Time-Out In Life

Have you ever felt that sometimes you are moving forward too far and too fast? If so, this phenomenon is natural. Many of us are usually caught up in the momentum and thrive on its excitement and energy without giving a second thought to the present moment or to looking back at how much we have gained and accomplished.

Perhaps today is a good time for us to slow down a little and take a break so that we will not miss out on a remarkable, quiet moment of contemplation and a personal time-out. Performing this delicate balance between pursuing our goals and standing still long enough to enjoy the fruits of our labors is an important and necessary step, as it essentially helps us to celebrate the positive happenings in our lives. It also allows us to regroup by giving us the opportunity to review our mission and make the necessary strategic refinements as needed.

Since we always have supporting casts—whether in our professional work life or in our personal life—this planned slowdown is long enough to give fellow teammates and loved ones the opportunity to catch up, and more importantly, it also creates a quality question-and-answer session for everyone involved.

According to my mom, Eleanora, *"When we view life as a never-ending race in itself, without the need to rush to the finish line, pacing ourselves along the way with the right time-outs, will only make the journey sweeter and more rewarding."*

As we travel on the highway of life, we will find that changes are never easy, and some changes may require making small sacrifices in order to gain a **_greater good_** in our respective lives.

Chapter 8

Coming to a Full Circle

While surfing the Internet years ago, I came upon this riddle/question, *"When a tortoise loses its shell, does it lose its home, or is it naked?"*

Unlike a turtle, a tortoise does and will always retreat into its shell when it senses danger approaching or when it doesn't want to be disturbed.

When we are cognizant of the above and accept that the shell is the tortoise's home where it feels safe and secure, we are correct.

However, if we were to accept that the shell is actually a special external skin for the tortoise and that home is actually the spot where it finally comes to rest, whether among some rocks or at the base of some trees, surrounded by other tortoises, we are also correct.

I believe both perspectives are correct if we put both our minds and our hearts to work. For some of us, home is where the heart is, regardless of where we are physically located. Whether we are in the company of family and friends or by ourselves, we are always comfortable as contentment comes from within us.

On the other hand, for some of us, home is where we are currently physically located. The feeling of security and comfort comes from being with family and friends. The synergy of belonging and community means a great deal to us.

As we and our parents grow older, these feelings of security and comfort become more prevalent in our respective lives as the changes in the natural cycle of human life occur. Not all of these changes will always be as smooth as we would like them to be.

Whether planned or unplanned, these changes will eventually put us in a paradigm shift of being a parent to our parents. For some of us, this shift will be gradual, but for some of us, it may be quite sudden, giving birth to the "sandwich generation." However, if we approach these changes with love, a twist of humility, and, at times, with lightheartedness and humor, we can almost assure ourselves of a positive outcome.

Having a genuine interest in our parents' well-being at heart, our teaching, coaching, counseling, and cheerleading abilities will now naturally come into play whenever we are needed to assist our parents in any situation that arises that requires a well-thought-out decision.

We are a teacher to our parents whenever we walk them through the transition of adapting and taking advantage of today's technology.

Johnny Tan

We don't have to look very hard to clearly see that every generation has its own advances in technology. Ask any of our moms, grandmas, and great-grandmas about their life in the kitchen, and they will be quick to walk you through their experiences of yesteryear, from wood-burning kitchen stoves to gas kitchen stoves to electric kitchen stoves and now, microwaves.

All of my friends were amazed when I told them that my then 91-year-old foster mom, Carol, was on the Internet every day. To top it off, a few years earlier, she actually blocked her nephew's email address because she was upset with his personal remarks and comments about some personal issues. Just imagining an 80-something-year-old taking command of her computer and blocking someone's email is enough to put a smile on your face!

We are a coach to our parents whenever we are there to give them support and encouragement when they encounter life's hits and misses that force them to make changes in their normal routines and lifestyles.

Like a mosaic, where the small pieces are critical to seeing the whole, a successful family is built by its members, who are focused on a vision of the family's preservation and the pursuit of the family's economic success and happiness.

By using conversations as the connective tissue that binds relationships together, past and current life lessons can be shared over time through the form of hilarious stories and personal anecdotes.

We are a counselor to our parents whenever we are there to listen, offer feedback, and give suggestions to them when they need to overcome personal fears or discomfort while transitioning from one aging phase of their lives to another.

Being mindful that they are still our parents, the success of our *counselorship* will come from our unique approach of taking advantage of the plethora of honesty available to us. This honesty is acquired by opening ourselves to feedback from our parents and realizing that reaching out for their opinion is not a sign that we do not know what to do; rather, we are simply taking advantage of the value of their thoughts and insights they are willing to share.

By listening without criticism and eventually integrating their ideas with our own views and experiences, we can then present and share these *"repackaged suggestions"* in a respectful way that will result in the validation of our overall child-parents/parents-child relationship synergy.

We are a cheerleader to our parents whenever we verbally express our joyful enthusiasm for their efforts in trying to accomplish something that may have been routine in the past for them but now seems to be a bit of a challenge because of their current physical and perhaps mental limitations. By remembering that they were the loudest cheerleaders for us at our various finish lines and how we felt at that time, well, it is our parent's turn to feel the overwhelming energy of *"unconditional love and support"* during their senior journey to living their best life.

As we travel on the highway of life, we will find that changes are never easy, and some changes may require making small sacrifices in order to gain a greater good in our respective lives. When we focus our energy on achieving this greater good, we will then recognize that sometimes *"being right can be wrong, and being wrong can be right."* This enlightenment is all about *"understanding and love."*

On the lighter side, always remember that the child in us will always teach the adult in us how to be happy for no reason, how to be always busy with something, and how to demand with all of our might that which we desire.

It is when we are fully engaged in this true synergy of family relationship dynamics that we finally *"Come To A Full Circle"* in our own life journey.

Dianne, Elsa Mae, Ginger, and I Celebrating First Release TV Interview

Finally, to truly understand *"Motherly Love"* is to truly understand that the greatest joy in life is in the creation of another human, that true love is putting another person's needs above ours, and that being happy does not mean that everything is perfect, but that, we have chosen to look beyond the imperfections.

Life's happiness is not a destination but rather the ***journey*** itself. Therefore, always **live to learn, to love, and to live a legacy.**

Chapter 9

My 9 MOMS
Conversations about Life, Love, and Laughter

I hope by now, some of the motherly wisdom and stories shared in the previous chapters have touched your heart and moved your soul. The most crucial life lesson I have learned from the various kitchen table conversations with my 9 MOMS about life, love, and laughter is that *"Real Wealth is not What We Accumulate. It Is What We Give Away!"* Everyone has their own interpretation of the word Wealth; mine is *"Knowledge, Wisdom, and Time."* I came to this realization of knowing that I still have much to offer others in need while navigating my life during times of paucity of funds. With authentic integrity, I am at my best when I share them with others. For me, contributing to someone's happiness, being a blessing in their life, and helping them experience the abundance of their highest self is *Joyful Living 360!*

Here are 9 new timeless recipes for living life from my 9 MOMS that profoundly contribute to the nourishment of my heart, mind, body, and spirit, especially during the last 15 years as I worked my way back up from the bottom of the Grand Canyon of Life. In my midst of feeling helpless, alone, and vulnerable, these transformational and empowering timeless motherly pearls of wisdom helped inspire me to never tap out emotionally but instead, dust off and prepare myself with enthusiasm to experience and flavor all that life has to offer as I reconstruct the *"new me!"*

1. Smiling Sows Happiness—My mom, Elsa Mae, is always all smiles! She taught me that *"A Smile is a Handshake that is Seldom Refused."* For someone known as a people person, I am actually shy and somewhat introverted. Although having mastered the six cornerstones of self-mastery collectively taught to me by my 9 Moms as I live in my bubble of quiet confidence, it would take a lot for me to initiate contact with others. However, once the connection is made, I am as bubbly as one can get.

The most important thing I learned about the power of *"Smiling"* is that it creates a positive, happy energy Aura around us. Others can consciously and subconsciously pick up on this energizing shift, which leads to happy, jovial interactions every time! By the way, if someone doesn't get your engaging positive vibes, it is their loss, not yours, as *"smiling sows happiness"* within first. This is the best, most effective, and timeless self-picker-upper.

2. Gratitude Cultivates Blessings—My mom, Eleanora, goes all out celebrating Thanksgiving every year with family and friends. She taught me, *"Being truly grateful for the gifts and positivity of life's offerings triggers even more blessings to come our way."* My first Thanksgiving experience at 19 years old impacted me tremendously. During dinner, we were asked to share what we were grateful for that year. It led me to truly understand and appreciate the power of *"Gratitude"* that we sometimes take for granted. Besides thanking my parents for their trust and support of me for being halfway around the world from them, I was extremely grateful to have Eleanora and her husband, Nick, as my host family.

Since then, every night, as I lay in bed before falling asleep, I always reflect upon the day's happenings, for which I am grateful. From a simple deed of holding a vestibule door open for someone who later returned the favor as we exchanged smiles and thanks to being grateful for getting the last can of crushed pineapple at the grocery store to complement my dinner recipe for the evening! It is the *"counting of my blessings moments"* for the day.

3. Generosity Reaps Abundance—My mom, Carol, taught me that generosity is not always about giving money. It is about sharing your *"Wealth"* to help others in their journey of building a better life for themselves and their families. At 20 years old, I wasn't sure what that really meant until later that summer, during my two-week semester break, while helping out at one of her restaurants, I gave an employee, who was in his 30s, a ride home one evening. I got to know him to be a friendly, reliable, and nice person during the couple of weeks of hanging out at the restaurant. When we arrived at his house, his mother was sitting on the front porch. She invited me in.

They were happy I accepted the invitation. However, they were also embarrassed as the interior was just plain with minimal furnishings. They explained that it was actually an abandoned house they had been fortunate to live in for the last six months. The owner left the area, knew the current unfortunate circumstances of a single mother and her son, and was kind enough to leave things as is! I have always been a generous giver to help others; however, while I was in the trenches working my way up from the bottom, I realized that I possess a far more valuable asset I can offer people besides money: my *"Knowledge, Wisdom, and Time,"* which with grace, have made a tremendous impact in building a better world for others to benefit from and follow!

Johnny Tan

4. Faith Comforts—My mom, Ginger, known for her favorite phrase, *"And The Good New Is..."* always managed to ignite the little spark within me whenever I needed to jumpstart myself again after being flattened out by life's challenges. The most profound moment was when I fell to the bottom of the Grand Canyon of Life due to unforeseen events and circumstances in my personal and professional life when I moved to Dallas, Texas. One evening, I called Ginger to share the latest happenings. She practically listened to me into existence. Some 45 minutes later, when I finally finished expressing myself, she began by saying three words: God Heard You. *"And The Good News Is... you realized where you are. Now, it is your time to do what you have always done so well, which is organizing and planning."*

She said, *"Johnny, have Faith because it is History! Look at all that you have accomplished out of the other life's challenges. The current situation is no different. Let the history of past successes comfort you as you regroup and refocus. Allow the empowering energy of Faith to comfort you as you write your new chapter in re-inventing yourself. Always remember, God loves you, and I love you, dear!"* With that, I felt her genuine, warm, loving, big, confident smile coming through my cell phone. Ginger's consoling and encouraging words alleviated the psychological weight that was paralyzing me. She just taught me how to use the power of *Faith*. Feeling drained but inspired, I slept well for the first time in many months.

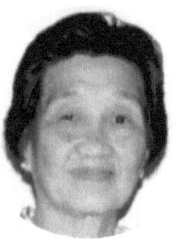

5. Hope Inspires—My mom, Nyah, taught my sister and me to never give up on anything we aspire to do and achieve because she believes the power of *"Hope"* will always get us over the finish line. The first time I fully embraced this powerful mindset was when I made it to the United States to attend college after graduating from high school at 17 years old in Melaka, Malaysia, just as my mom had assured me I would. Since then, the word has been my guiding flashlight whenever I need assistance to achieve a goal that may initially look unattainable. After my dad's sudden passing in my sophomore year, *"Hope"* was all I had to inspire and guide me as I continued with my life's journey in the U.S.

It led me to meet eight incredible women who became my surrogate moms. Collectively, my 9 Moms constantly reminded me of the power of *"Hope"* as I pursue my life's dreams and desires. They are right! I recall many a time, just when I thought I was out for the count, I was able to muster enough strength and courage to push forward, as each day, *"Hope"* provided me with a fresh, clean sheet of paper to start over and create, plan, act, and not give up! Over the years, despite experiencing plenty of unexpected tearful setbacks, the unwavering power of *"Hope"* inspired me every morning, which eventually led me to various successful rebounds and arriving at my highest self!

Johnny Tan

6. Love Empowers—My mom, Dianne, is all about *"Love"*—love for ballroom dancing, love for your neighbor, love for your friends. She taught me a new perspective on *"Love"* when we discussed how she spent so much time with a casual neighbor who was living her final months with terminal cancer. I learned that looking through the lens of *"Love"* at a person or situation allows us to focus on the beauty in others and the infinite possibilities that lie ahead. It helps us look for what is right instead of wrong and draws out the best in others and ourselves.

Expressing our *"Love"* comes next, and there are two ways: verbal and nonverbal communication. Both versions empower people; however, the nonverbal expressions often speak louder than verbal ones. This revelation moved me in ways I never could have imagined. It provided me the quiet confidence to exercise my natural emphatic nature when crossing paths with individuals who needed more than a warm, comforting assurance that a new tomorrow begins when the sun rises the following day.

When we view every circumstance as the cusp of a new beginning, we embrace the idea that every moment is a *Conscious Choice*. Happiness, joy, and harmony soon follow when we allow the empowering vision of *"Love"* to cultivate the wholeness of the heart, mind, body, and spirit experience. I now understand that it is the nature of true *"Love"* that nourishes the power of Relationships, as it reveals the real meaning of Life.

7. Always Lean Towards Heaven—My mom, Toni, approaches life by living in the moment. She believes that crying over spilled milk doesn't change anything except sucking away our energy from the here and now. As far as tomorrow is concerned, well, let's just say that when dawn arrives, hallelujah! So, *"today"* is the most precious time we have, as she taught me her signature 3Ps - planning, playing, and praying!

> **Planning because** - well, with God's grace, we have another day to live!
>
> **Playing because** - today may be the only day we have. So, take it out for a full spin to enjoy yourself, and do not hold back by trying to save something for another day!
>
> **Praying because** - we are all spiritual beings, and achieving our desires, whether through manifestation or self-creation, may require the touch of divine magic. As such, always remind yourself, *"Regardless of Where You Are in Life, Always Lean Towards Heaven,"* as this is the spiritual grounding that will give us the assurance of tranquility and confidence that

everything happens in *"Divine Timing"* for our greatest good!

Over the years, and especially in the last 15 formidable ones, I have experienced several *"Divine Timing"* events that helped validate and strengthen my spiritual beliefs. I now live with tranquility and confidence, knowing that divine magic is only a prayer mindset away.

8. Passion is When the Heart Creates the Mind Formulates— My mom, Betty, always uses passion to complete her to-do list. She is an excellent organizer and was instrumental in introducing ballroom dancing to the community when she first moved to Baton Rouge, Louisiana. She also successfully created and coordinated numerous ballroom dance events to benefit causes such as the American Cancer Society and the rescue workers in the 9-11 WTC tragedy, to name a few.

Betty taught me a fresh perspective on goal setting and planning. She believes that any project created from a heart-centered approach will always energize our minds to formulate all the ways to accomplish it with passion. She is right! Although I achieved all the personal and professional goals I had set for myself prior to meeting her, the accomplished experience was somewhat flat because they were tasks I needed to get done; in short, "Yeah, I made it!" Shifting my taskmaster perspective to a heart-centered approach immediately helped me experience a more relaxed and engaging fun mindset.

The *"new me"* radiates a contagious joyful enthusiasm, benefiting everyone involved in the various projects. I learned that when our actions are an extension of our hearts, they create a *"mindful expression" on the Canvas of Life!* Whether it is for our family, friends, or collaborative partners, if we want to leave a *Legacy of Love* for others, taking time to create with our Heart and letting our Mind plan how to achieve it assures the synergistic wholeness experience of the heart, mind, body, and spirit!

9. Wisdom is about knowing Others. Enlightenment is about knowing Ourselves—My mom, Dee, is a highly intuitive lady. Originally from Madera, PA, she lived in Moshannon, PA, before moving to Houston, TX. Dee helped me understand that wisdom is acquired not only from the life experiences we encounter ourselves but also from the people we meet and interact with.

Given the opportunity to speak, everyone has something to share—the good, the bad, and the ugly. This information gives a complete picture of the person, the situations they have encountered in their life's journey, and their final summation of these experiences. According to Dee, regardless of how we meet these individuals, whether through our personal or professional circles, the knowledge gained from them contributes to our personal enlightenment.

Since embracing Dee's methodology, I have experienced transformational personal growth while educating myself about life and living. I realized that engaging people with a genuine desire to learn helped me connect with them on a deeper level and, most importantly, facilitated me in making thorough and informed decisions whenever the situation arises.

One of the greatest successes I accomplished was in my first career in leadership and management as the COO of a 600+ multi-generation workforce at 33 years old. I utilized my enlightened understanding that *"We are in the People Business. We lead people, and we manage situations."* This refined *"corporate family culture employee engagement"* program I created helped us retain highly skilled people in our organization, leading to rapid growth and expansion benefiting everyone.

While on my enlightenment journey, I discovered that I am an Autodidact, a Manifesting Generator, and a Sigma male. I learned from everyday people from all walks of life because I am always open to learning something new. I perceive what others may consider mundane as new information that may come in handy one day. I have also been fortunate for the last 15 years to connect with and gain tremendous knowledge from the various guests I hosted on my From My Mama's Kitchen® Talk Radio show.

What started as a live internet radio show to complement the original book, with a mission of providing listeners with a resource center vibrant with motivational, inspirational, and spiritual stories from guests of ordinary people doing extraordinary feats and instilling a positive attitude in our global community, soon became a personal, educational platform for me to acquire knowledge and wisdom from my superlative guests. Our kitchen table conversation topics address family matters, relationships, community diversity, personal growth, health and wellness, spirituality, and conscious living. The show has amassed over one million listeners.

In addition to sharing their remarkable life journeys, my radio guests also shared their recipes for living life in every show. Here is a snippet of past guests I had the honor to interview: International luminaries like Dr. Ervin Laszlo, twice nominated for the Nobel Peace Prize; the inventor/father of the cell phone, Martin Cooper; and world-renowned master teacher of Feng Shui and the law of attraction, and an international bestselling author, Marie Diamond. Other luminaries included the New York Times bestselling authors Christy Whitman, Bernie Seigel MD, and Gay Hendricks; the #1 New York Times bestselling author Carol Kline; international bestselling author Sandra Biskind; and Amy Newmark, publisher and editor-in-chief of Chicken Soup for the Soul.

I am so thankful Dee taught me how to utilize the University of Life. Enlightenment, in essence, is *"Self-Mastery."* It leads to *"Conscious Action."* What follows is that *"It is not about what happened; it is about how we respond to what happened."* As we navigate this path, we remind ourselves that self-expression is a unique journey—

one where we are not seeking validation but rather embracing the liberating nature of sharing our true selves without constraints.

When we let our voice express our individuality and the beauty of personal authenticity with integrity, we foster an environment of open dialogue within. We create a space where expectations align, misunderstandings dissipate, and connections flourish with a renewed sense of harmony and understanding—*Our Bubble of Quiet Confidence*. When wisdom synergizes with enlightenment, we experience intellectual power. This gift of aligning our heart, mind, body, and spirit produces boundless joy, an abundance of selflessness, and divine luck. My journey of enlightenment has led me to speak and teach that *"personal success begins at home within our authentic selves."* Embracing this new perspective leads us to joyfully *"Live and Perform in Our Genius Zone."*

Final Food for Thought for this 15th Anniversary Special Edition

I hope reading this book has helped you reflect back and rekindle the many insightful words of wisdom that were shared with you over the years during heartfelt moments that somehow have been forgotten.

My sister, Rosalind, sent me this insightful reminder a few years ago as a Lunar New Year well wishes. I would like to share them with you as a final serving from our kitchen table to yours.

- **Health** makes all things possible.
- **Wealth** makes all things work.
- **Love** makes all things beautiful.
- **May You Have All Three.**

Since this book is designed as a heart-centered keepsake, the following pages are for you to write down **"The Recipe(s) for Living"** your mom(s) taught you or perhaps the ones you would like to share with your loved ones when you give this book as a **Gift!**

Mama's Recipe for Living

www.FromMyMamasKitchen.com

Mama's Recipe for Living

www.FromMyMamasKitchen.com

Mama's Recipe for Living

Since my original intention for From My Mama's Kitchen book was a keepsake collection of my mamas's food recipes, I have included 9 of my favorite recipes for you.

Bon Appétit!

Food Recipes

Recipes from Eleanora Carter

Roast Leg of Lamb

5 - 6 pound leg of lamb
1 clove garlic, cut into slivers
salt and pepper

Wipe lamb thoroughly with a damp towel. Sprinkle with salt and pepper. Make slits in the meat and insert slivers of garlic into the meat. Place lamb on rack in shallow roasting pan. Roast in a 325-degree oven for 2 1/2 hours or 20 minutes per pound.

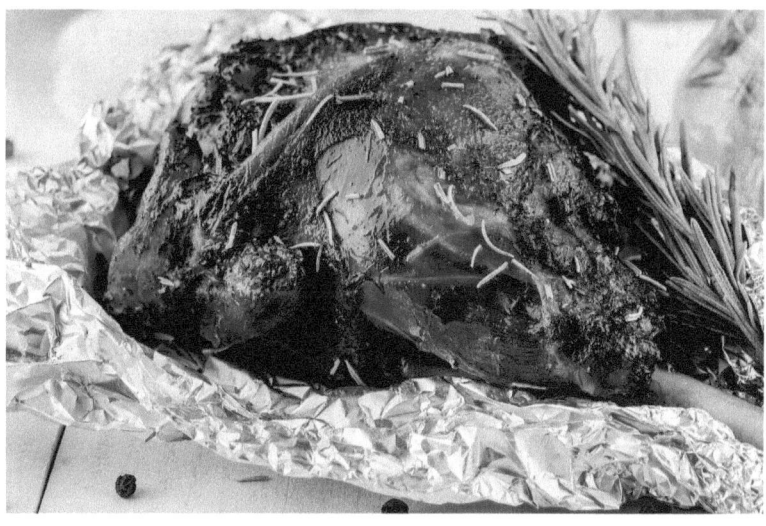

Oyster Dressing

1/2 cup butter or margarine
2 eggs, slightly beaten
2 large onions, minced
3 cloves garlic, minced
1/2 bunch green onions, minced
4 teaspoons minced parsley
1 bay leaf
3 doz. small oysters, cut in half
1 sprig of thyme
2 teaspoons salt
1/2 cup celery, minced
1/4 teaspoon black pepper
1 loaf stale French bread, cut into small cubes
warm water

Melt butter or margarine in a 10-inch skillet. Sauté onions, bay leaf, thyme, and celery; cook until tender over low heat (about 20 minutes). Add garlic, parsley, and oysters; cook until almost all of the water leaves oysters (about 15 minutes). Remove bay leaf and thyme. Soak the bread in warm water. Squeeze water out of bread. Add to oyster mixture. Stir and cook until thoroughly heated (about 15 minutes). Remove from heat; add salt, pepper and eggs. Mix well. Stuffing is enough for a ten-pound turkey.

Praline Yam Casserole

4 medium yams cooked and peeled
1/2 cup dark brown sugar
or 2 1-pound 4-ounce cans
1/3 cup melted butter
2 eggs, beaten
1 teaspoon salt
1/2 cup pecan halves

Peel and quarter yams. Boil until tender. Drain and mash. Combine yams with eggs, 1/4 cup of brown sugar, 2 tablespoons of melted butter, and salt. Place the mixture in a 1-quart casserole. Arrange pecan halves in a pattern over the top. Sprinkle with the remaining 1/4 cup brown sugar and drizzle with the remaining butter. Bake uncovered in a 375-degree oven for 20 minutes. Dish serves 8.

Recipes from Carol Wisdom

Chicken and Dumplings

Cook chicken and de-bone and cut it into small pieces. Put celery, carrots, and onions into the broth.

Make Dumplings

1 cup of flour
1 egg
1 cup of the above broth
1 teaspoon of salt
1 teaspoon of baking powder

Make Stiff Dough

Roll out 1/8" thick, cut into strips of 3" long, and drop into boiling broth. Optional: You can also add milk to the broth for a different enhanced flavor.

Pecan Coconut Pie

3 Eggs
2/3 Cup of Sugar
1/2 Tea Spoon of Salt
1/3 Cup of Butter or Oleo melted
1 Cup of Corn Syrup
1 Cup of Pecan Halves
2/3 Cup of Coconut

Beat the ingredients together and mix in pecan and coconut. Pour mixture into a pastry shell.

Pre-heat oven. Bake at 375 degrees for 40 to 45 minutes. Serve with cool whip or ice cream.

Recipe from Dianne Heise

Breaded Veal Cutlet (Wiener Schnitzel)

1 center-cut veal steak
1 egg (beaten)
2 tablespoons milk
soda crackers (finely crushed) hydrogenated lard
flour
salt
black pepper

Cut the veal into several individual pieces. Trim off any skin or gristle. (The steak should not be more than 1/4 inch thick.) Pound the pieces with a wooden mallet to tenderize them. Stir the milk into the beaten egg. Dredge the veal in the egg-milk mixture and then in the cracker crumbs. Melt lard in an iron skillet. Fry veal a few pieces at a time until golden brown.

Place in an oven-proof container until all the veal is browned. Place the open container in a 300 F oven & roast until tender (approximately 30 minutes).

A sauce (gravy) can be prepared by adding flour to the pan drippings and stirring until there are no lumps. Add water to get the desired consistency. Bring to a simmer. Add salt and pepper to taste. This sauce can be served over mashed potatoes. A side dish that goes well with this meal is cooked carrots and peas. It should be noted that soda crackers are also called 'saltines.' It should also be noted that this is not a low-cholesterol meal! A dessert that is often served with this traditional German meal is cooked and chilled Farina (cream-of-wheat), which is like a stiff pudding served with raspberry sauce.

Recipe from Ginger White

Frank's Shrimp Cocodrie

1/2 stick of real butter
3 tablespoons bacon drippings
1 cup thinly sliced green onions
1/2 cup finely chopped celery
4 cloves finely chopped garlic
1 cup finely crumbled bacon
1/2 cup white wine
1/2 cup reduced shrimp stock
2 bottles Catalina french dressing (16 oz. size)
2 lemons, juiced and seeded
1 tablespoon creole mustard
3 tablespoons Worcestershire sauce
2 tablespoons Louisiana hot sauce
1 2oz. package Philadelphia cream cheese
1 cup Velveeta cheese, cubed
4 lbs. peeled and deveined shrimp (16-20 count)
1/2 cup finely chopped parsley
salt and cayenne pepper to taste

In a 12-inch skillet, sauté onions, celery, and garlic in the butter and bacon drippings over "medium heat" until they soften, but do not let the garlic brown. Then pour in the wine and shrimp stock and bring the heat to "medium-high." Cook until the alcohol is reduced and the seasoning and the vegetables blend into the stock, approximately five to seven minutes.

Stir in the dressing, reduce the heat to "low," and simmer the mixture until the vinegar aroma is just about gone. Gradually add one ingredient at a time, stirring in Creole mustard, Worcestershire, and hot sauce until the mixture is thoroughly blended. Continue to simmer for about five minutes.

Stir the two cheeses into the mixture and dissolve them thoroughly. When the mixture is creamy and smooth (with the consistency of melted ice cream), stir in the parsley. Place all the shrimp in an 11 x 17 baking pan. Pour the mixture over the shrimp (you want to make sure the shrimp are almost covered with the sauce so that they can bake evenly).

Place the baking pan on the center rack of a 400-degree pre-heated oven and bake uncovered for about 8 to 10 minutes (or until the shrimp are pink and the sauce is hot and bubbly.) Be careful not to overcook the shrimp, as they will turn tough and rubbery.

When the shrimp are just tender, remove them from the oven. Ladle them (along with a generous helping of the sauce) into a warm bowl and serve.

Recipe from Elsa Mae Stevens

Pound Cake

2 sticks butter
3 cups sugar
1/2 teaspoon baking powder
1 cup milk
1/2 cup shortening (Crisco)
5 eggs
3 cups plain flour
1/2 teaspoon salt
2 teaspoons vanilla

Cream shortening, add sugar, and mix well.

Beat in the eggs one at a time.

Combine flour, baking powder, and salt.

Add in alternate proportion with milk and mix. Add flavoring last.

Pour mixture into a greased and floured tube or loaf pan and bake at 325 degrees for 1 1/2 hours.

Pound Cake

Malaysian Chicken and Quail Eggs Curry

Recipe from Nyah Tan

Malaysian Chicken and Quail Eggs Curry

2 pounds of chicken cut into bite-size pieces
4 potatoes, quartered
1 can of quail eggs rinsed (15 oz. can)
1 1/2 cup coconut milk
6 tablespoons curry powder (mixed with water into a paste)
2 cinnamon sticks
2 – 3 stalks of curry leaves
1 – 2 star anise
1 teaspoon minced ginger
1 1/2 tablespoons minced garlic
1 1/2 tablespoons minced red onion
7 tablespoons of cooking oil

Sauté the red onion, garlic, ginger, cinnamon sticks, star anise, and curry leaves in a 5-quart pot over medium-high heat for 3 to 4 minutes. Add the curry paste and continue to stir/sauté the mixture for 5 to 7 minutes.

Add the chicken and stir the mixture for 2 minutes. Add the coconut milk and stir the mixture until it comes to a soft boil. Add the potatoes, quail eggs, and 3 cups of water, reduce heat to medium, and cook covered for 5 minutes. Add salt to taste, and continue to let the dish simmer over low heat for another 3 to 5 minutes. Serve over rice or pasta.

About the Author

Like a pot of the famous Louisiana gumbo, Johnny Tan's life has been richly flavored by his 9 Moms over the years. His life experiences have led him to the top of his personal Mount Everest and also falling to the bottom of the Grand Canyon of Life.

In April 2007, Johnny began recording the many heartfelt words of motherly wisdom from his 9 Moms' kitchen table conversations. The result was the 2009 release of From My Mama's Kitchen—"food for the soul, recipes for living."

Adopted at birth in Melaka, Malaysia, Johnny arrived in the United States at 18 to attend LSU in Baton Rouge, Louisiana. Here, his life's journey led him to cross paths with several ladies he affectionately referred to as moms. They provided inspiration, emotional support, and life skills, guiding him in pursuing personal and professional excellence.

After college, Johnny worked in the restaurant industry for 18 years.

In 2001, he left a successful career as a chief operating officer to pursue his dream of owning a business. He started The Reyna Collection®, a premier multi-line resource group at the Dallas Market Center representing several major companies and manufacturers. Its diverse product line includes architectural antiques, bronze sculptures and figurines, and custom-designed water features.

Johnny's third career began when his heart-centered and passion-driven book, From My Mama's Kitchen—"food for the soul, recipes for living," honoring his 9 moms won five awards and became a bestseller.

Today, Johnny is an experiential keynote speaker, executive career and life coach, mentor, talk show host, publisher of Inspirations for Better Living, and owner of the WordsHavePower.store. As a social entrepreneur, he is the founder and CEO of From My Mama's Kitchen®, a non-profit 501c3 organization. Its mission is to help people design their lives with the power of resilience to live and perform in their "Genius Zone" through From My Mama's Kitchen® Genius Zone Educational Platform Community Enrichment Programs.

In 2021, the prestigious Global Forum for Education and Learning (GFEL) awarded Johnny one of the Top 100 Visionaries in Education, and in 2022, he was an invited Executive Contributor to Global BRAINZ Magazine.

Driven by his personal and professional core values (on his websites), Johnny is committed to enriching the lives of everyone he meets. He uses his leadership skills to advocate "Personal Success Begins at Home," supporting people and bolstering their spirits for the good of the community to build a better world and leave a legacy of love.

Johnny is also an accomplished ballroom dance performer and teacher. He has performed with his dance partners for years at various ballroom and charity events in Louisiana and Texas.

Please visit the following websites to learn more about Johnny, From My Mama's Kitchen®, and to get updates on upcoming events:

www.JoyfulLiving360.com
www.FromMyMamasKitchen.com
www.FromMyMamasKitchen.org

A celebration of the
heart with a gift from
the soul.

Dear Readers,

Thank you for reading my book. I hope the wonderful memories it brought back helped to put a smile on your face and a feeling of laughter and joy in your heart.

Please join me in sharing the power of *"unconditional motherly love"* by writing a short review expressing your feelings about the book. You can post your review wherever you purchased this heart-centered and passion-driven book.

Your testimonial will validate the book's inspiring and empowering message as we collectively build a better world for others to benefit from and follow. Your participation will help us reach other readers.

Again, thank you for your support and assistance in joining our team in *"Leaving a Legacy of Love."*

With gratitude and blessings always,

Johnny Tan